Fighting for the United States, Executed in Britain

Fighting for the United States, Executed in Britain

US Soldiers Court-Martialled in WWII

Simon Webb

Pen & Sword

MILITARY

AN IMPRINT OF PEN & SWORD BOOKS LTD.
YORKSHIRE – PHILADELPHIA

First published in Great Britain in 2021 by
Pen & Sword Military
An imprint of
Pen & Sword Books Ltd
Yorkshire - Philadelphia

ISBN 978 1 52679 095 8

Printed and bound in England
By CPI Group (UK) Ltd, Croydon, CR0 4YY

Pen & Sword Books Ltd incorporates the Imprints of Pen & Sword Archaeology,
Atlas, Aviation, Battleground, Discovery, Family History, History, Maritime,
Military, Naval, Politics, Railways, Select, Transport, True Crime, Fiction,
Frontline Books, Leo Cooper, Praetorian Press, Seaforth Publishing,
Wharncliffe and White Owl.

For a complete list of Pen & Sword titles please contact

PEN & SWORD BOOKS LIMITED
47 Church Street, Barnsley, South Yorkshire, S70 2AS, England
E-mail: enquiries@pen-and-sword.co.uk
Website: www.pen-and-sword.co.uk

or

PEN AND SWORD BOOKS
1950 Lawrence Rd, Havertown, PA 19083, USA
E-mail: uspen-and-sword@casematepublishers.com
Website: www.penandswordbooks.com

MIX
Paper from
responsible sources
FSC
www.fsc.org
FSC® C013604

Contents

List of Illustrations

1. Thomas Jefferson, the founding father of America whose policies affected the treatment of American soldiers in Britain during the Second World War.
2. A section of seventeenth-century stonework at Shepton Mallet Prison.
3. The execution of the conspirators involved in Abraham Lincoln's assassination.
4. An X-ray of the so-called hangman's fracture.
5. The 'cowboy coil' noose favoured by American executioners.
6. The free-running noose used in British hangings of the twentieth century.
7. The table of drops used to calculate the distance the prisoner should fall in British executions.
8. The new execution building constructed by the Americans when they took over Shepton Mallet Prison in 1942.
9. The cramped execution chamber; the railings mark the spot where the trapdoor once was.
10. The remains of the hinges of the trapdoors, still visible on the rafters below the modern floorboards.
11. Thomas Pierrepoint; by the time he undertook the executions of American soldiers, he was in his seventies.
12. Albert Pierrepoint, Thomas Pierrepoint's nephew and his assistant at most of the hangings carried out at Shepton Mallet.
13. Lee Davis, the first man to be executed for rape in Britain for over a century.

Introduction

In January 1942 the first American forces arrived in Britain to join the fight against Nazi Germany. A month earlier, the surprise attack on their naval base at Pearl Harbor had precipitated the involvement of the United States in what was now a world war. Shortly after the Japanese assault on Pearl Harbor, Germany declared war on America, with the result that America and Britain became allies, fighting for the liberation of Europe. Between 1942 and 1945, the year that the Second World War ended, a total of ninety-six American servicemen were executed after being tried by courts martial, eighty-nine by hanging and seven by firing squads. Of these men, eighteen were executed in England. Another American soldier, Karl Hulten, was hanged in London's Pentonville Prison after a trial in a British court; the rest were executed at Shepton Mallet Prison, in the English county of Somerset. This, the oldest prison in England, had been provided to the US Army as a disciplinary establishment.

A peculiarity of the hangings carried out at Shepton Mallet when it was under the control of the United States was that they were all undertaken by British executioners, the British government having forbidden the US Army from hanging anybody in their country. There was no objection to firing squads, but executions by hanging had to be conducted by the British themselves. This was odd, because the armed forces of the United States were in all other respects quite literally a law unto themselves. An Act of Parliament was passed which prevented any American soldier from being prosecuted in the United Kingdom for any crime at all, including murder, unless the agreement of the United States government had been obtained. Despite having given America and its armed forces freedom from the law of the land

and allowing them to run their own affairs precisely as they wished, why should Britain stand resolute and inflexible on this one, relatively insignificant point? How could the nationality of the man who operated the gallows by pulling a lever possibly matter that much? To answer that question will require a detailed and lengthy examination of the process of judicial hanging.

It is no exaggeration to say that over the course of a century or so, the British had turned hanging people into an art. The aim, invariably achieved, was to snap the neck of the condemned man or woman cleanly, causing instant death. This was not a skill which the Americans had mastered and as late as 1930, a woman's head was wrenched from her body during an execution in the United States, landing at the feet of the horrified witnesses. More common was the situation when no damage at all was done to the neck and the victim simply choked to death at the end of the rope, a process which could take up to half an hour. We shall be studying the development of judicial hanging in both Britain and the United States, to see why the British government were inflexible on this one point.

In this book we shall also be examining the strange circumstances which led to American soldiers in Britain being immune from prosecution. To do so, we must look in some detail at the origins of the United States and how the country came to have a mortal dread of treaties and formal alliances. It will also be necessary to address the uncomfortable fact that although only 10 per cent of the United States forces in Britain were black, the majority of those executed at Shepton Mallet were black or of Hispanic origin. To understand why that should have been the case, the application of the death penalty in the United States itself must be scrutinized. Finally, we will explore the personal histories of all the nineteen American soldiers executed in Britain following courts martial or, in the case of Karl Hulten, a criminal trial in a British court. Hulten's case was the one exception to the rule above, that American soldiers committing crimes in Britain should be dealt with only by American courts martial, rather than the country's ordinary judicial system. In February 1946 the magazine *Tribune* published an essay by George Orwell, who was of course later to achieve fame as the author of *Nineteen Eighty-Four* and *Animal Farm*. Orwell's piece, entitled, 'Decline of the English Murder', was inspired by what became known as the 'Cleft Chin Murder'. This killing was carried out by Karl Hulten and his teenage girlfriend and because it involved a British citizen facing a capital charge, the United States government agreed that the interests of justice would be better served if the pair were tried in a British court, the only occasion on which an American serviceman faced a British court during the Second World War.

Of the nineteen American soldiers who were executed in Britain during the Second World War, all but two were hanged. The two who were not hanged were shot by firing squads. Eight were executed for murder, eight for rape and three for both murder and rape. This resulted in two curious historical anomalies. First, nobody had been executed for rape alone in Britain for over a century. It meant that a British executioner would be hanging men for an offence which in Britain would merit only a prison sentence. The second anomaly was that the British, although keen enough on firing squads during the First World War, had by the time the Americans arrived in the country in 1942 abandoned their use. One spy was executed by this method in January 1941, but those subsequently convicted of spying were all hanged. This means that the last executions by firing squad to be carried out in the British Isles also took place at Shepton Mallet.

We shall also be looking at the final disposal of the corpses of those who were executed in this way. All were initially buried in England, but were then moved to France. One or two then ended up back in the United States.

The story of the American soldiers executed in Britain during the Second World War is a fascinating one, touching as it does upon so many curious points of the history of both Britain and the United States. We must begin with the founding of the United States at the end of the eighteenth century, because unless we fully understand the horror which was felt at that time for what Thomas Jefferson described as 'entangling alliances', it will not be possible to make sense of what happened in 1942, when the United States joined the Second World War as an ally of Britain against Nazi Germany. Before doing so, a few words about capital punishment in Britain might not come amiss, because nobody under the age of 65 or 70 is likely to remember anything of the time that people were regularly being hanged in English and Scottish prisons.

In the United States, executions are of course still a regular occurrence in parts of the country. Perhaps twenty people a year are executed in America by means of lethal injections. In Britain, on the other hand, it is almost 60 years since an execution took place and what was once an integral part of the country's culture has all but faded from memory. For many British readers of this book, the idea that there was once time when as many people were being hanged in London, Liverpool, Manchester and Edinburgh as die each year in the United States by the death penalty is a strange and disturbing one. In 1954, for instance, seventeen men and one woman were hanged in the United Kingdom. The practice finally ended only in the 1960s. The last two men to be hanged in Britain died at the same time, in separate prisons, on 13 August 1964.

It is necessary to bear in mind that the subject of this book, although it might at first sight appear to be an historical curiosity, was once a common practice across the whole of the civilized world. Many of the incidents described have counterparts in the more recent world of the 1960s. In Chapter 3, for example, we look at an allegation which was circulating to the effect that those in the streets around Shepton Mallet Prison could actually hear the operation of the gallows in 1926, when the last civilian execution was carried out there. Then, in 1944, a similar tale was doing the rounds in the town about the firing squads which despatched two soldiers that year, that the sound of their executions was audible to people in the town. This fascination with witnessing, even vicariously, the moment of death for a condemned prisoner was once very common, not only in Shepton Mallet but throughout the whole country.

In the early 1960s, executions in Britain were invariably conducted at 9:00 am and schoolchildren were well aware of this. They heard their parents talking about this or that man who was to be hanged and when they were at school, their eyes would sometimes turn to the clock on the wall, telling them of the exact moment that a man was being done to death. It was an awful state of affairs. It needs to be borne in mind though that hanging in the days when the executions listed took place was just another unremarkable feature of everyday life.

Chapter 1

The Americans Arrive

On 30 October 1940, a few days before the American people voted to give him an unprecedented third term as President of the United States, Franklin D. Roosevelt addressed a large meeting in Boston. A bitter war had for the past year been raging in Europe, and it served to remind people in America of the more than 100,000 young men from their own country who had died in Europe, fighting in the First World War. The great fear was that a little over 20 years later, the United States might be about to become embroiled in another European war. Anxious to reassure them, the president made a categorical pledge that nothing of the kind would ever happen again;

> And while I am talking to you, mothers and fathers, I give you one more assurance. I have said this before, but I shall say it again and again and again: your boys are not going to be sent into any foreign wars.

On 26 January 1942, just 15 months after that speech, the first American troops arrived in Britain to take part in the biggest 'foreign war' the world had ever seen.

There was no contradiction between President Roosevelt's apparent determination to keep America from becoming involved in the war between Britain and Germany and the fact that he later felt obliged to conscript the citizens of his country and despatch them overseas to take part in what had by then become a worldwide war. To understand what happened, it will be necessary to go back to the very beginning of the United States, and the circumstances in which this new nation came into being.

When America declared its independence from Britain in 1776, it was not just from Britain that it wished to detach itself, but the whole quarrelsome bunch of nations which made up the continent of Europe. The new republic viewed with bewilderment the seemingly endless wars which had been tearing Europe apart for over a thousand years and were determined that they would forge an entirely different kind of polity, one which would not become involved in European affairs at all other than to trade. Just to put this desire to give Europe a wide berth in context, in the century which saw the founding of the United States, there had been a succession of wars across Europe. In 1700 the Great Northern War in the Baltic began, between Sweden and Russia. It lasted over 20 years. The following year saw the start of the War of the Spanish Succession, in which Britain was involved. This dragged on for a dozen years. In 1740 came the War of the Austrian Succession, followed a few years later by the Seven Years War and then, hot on its heels, the Russo-Turkish War, which only ended in 1774, two years before the American Declaration of Independence. Little wonder then that America was determined not to be dragged into any of these, to them, pointless and irrelevant disputes.

Rightly or wrongly, the Americans concluded that the main cause of this seemingly endless series of wars fought in Europe was the treaties and agreements which were made between the different countries. Because of these, one country might promise to come to the aid of another in time of war, which inevitably meant that what began as a disagreement between two countries could spread rapidly to draw in half a dozen others. Looking forward a little to the time with which this book is chiefly concerned, the Second World War, we observe that this was precisely how Britain became dragged into a war with Germany. Britain had guaranteed Poland's safety and when Germany attacked the country, the British felt duty-bound to come to the aid of Poland. Had it not been for that agreement, which also drew France into a war against Germany, then the Second World War might have been averted, at least in Europe.

Steering clear of formal alliances with other nations seemed, to the new nation which America had now become, to bring with it the promise of remaining independent and unfettered in their foreign policy. As Thomas Jefferson, the third President of the United States, put it so succinctly; 'Peace, commerce, and honest friendship with all nations – entangling alliances with none.' Illustration 1 shows Jefferson, whose policies led ultimately to the peculiar situation during the Second World War where American soldiers in Britain were immune from the laws which applied to everybody else.

The early years of America's existence as an independent nation must have convinced them of the wisdom of their decision to stay clear of Europe and its 'entangling alliances'. After the French Revolution, a coalition of European countries launched a war against the republic which had replaced the French monarchy and this segued seamlessly into the Napoleonic Wars which racked much of the world for the first years of the nineteenth century. The fighting took place from Scandinavia to South Africa, from the Caribbean to the Middle East, making this the first true world war. Britain managed to involve America in the business, by blockading ports in search of French shipping, an action which led to the Anglo-American War of 1812–14, which saw the British landing in America and burning Washington. All of this prompted James Monroe, who became president in 1817, to set out what was to become known as the Monroe Doctrine. This was contained in the annual message to Congress delivered in December 1823 and became the blueprint for American foreign policy for the next century or so.

European countries had a number of colonies in both North and South America during the nineteenth century, including British possessions such as Jamaica and Spanish ones like Cuba. As a result of a revolt in the Spanish colonies, there was a threat of military intervention from Europe. President Monroe made it plain that the United States would not tolerate any interference by European powers in any part of the Americas. Specifically, it was said that any attempt by a European nation to extend its influence in the Americas would be regarded by the United States as a threat to its own peace and security. The same would apply to the establishment of any new colonies, although the United States would tolerate those which already existed. An assurance was also given that not only would the United States not involve itself in the affairs of existing European colonies in that part of the world, but also it would not participate in any purely European wars.

For almost a century after it was first propounded, the Monroe Doctrine formed the cornerstone of American foreign policy. The Atlantic Ocean acted as a *cordon sanitaire*, protecting America from the contagion of the tribal politics which were felt to bedevil Europe. This determination to keep clear of wars or even binding treaties with European nations became known as isolationism and although the term is sometimes used in connection with countries other than the United States, isolationism is most often thought of as an American tendency. It was still a powerful trend in 1940, when Roosevelt gave the speech quoted at the beginning of this chapter.

American isolationism really meant avoiding European affairs and so instead of concerning themselves with what was happening to the east, the energies and interests of the United States turned west during the nineteenth century, first occupying and colonizing the vast and sparsely populated part of the North American continent which lay between Canada and Mexico, and then onwards, into the Pacific. So it was that as the century drew on, the Pacific Ocean became viewed as part of the United States' sphere of influence, just as the Atlantic was Britain's. By 1900, American influence reached as far as the Philippines, which lay on the edge of the South China Sea.

This then was the state of play in 1914, when Europe once again exploded, with a war being fought between Germany, Austria-Hungary and the Ottoman Empire against Russia, France and Britain. The Monroe Doctrine dictated that this was no concern of the United States and that as long as this new war was confined to Europe, then it would be a matter for Europe to settle. The then president, Woodrow Wilson, was in no doubt about America's position, saying on 19 August 1914, 'The United States must be neutral in fact as well as in name'. Two things happened to overturn this view and cause America to abandon its traditional stance and join in the war in Europe.

Britain being an island nation, it struck Germany that once mobile warfare in Belgium and France had ground to a halt on the Western Front, one way of defeating their enemy would be to starve them by instituting a blockade. Napoleon had tried something similar with his Continental System a hundred years earlier. This time though, Germany had at its disposal a weapon of which Napoleon could not have dreamed. The *Unterseeboot*, or under-sea boat, was a deadly innovation which changed the rules of naval warfare forever. With their U-boats, fast and efficient submarines, the Germans could cruise the North Sea and Atlantic, invisible to shipping on the surface, and then strike at will. A good deal of Britain's food was being imported from North America during the First World War and by striking at merchant ships from Canada and the United States, it was hoped that it would be possible to bring Britain to her knees and force her to sue for peace. It was a ruthless policy which very nearly succeeded.

There was one great drawback to Germany's policy of attacking merchant ships, rather than limiting itself to military targets, and that was that it ran the risk of drawing the United States into the war on Britain's side. As early as May 1915, the sinking of the passenger liner *Lusitania*, with the loss of 1,198 lives, over 100 of them Americans, caused great anger in the United States. Matters were not helped in early 1917, when German Foreign Secretary Arthur Zimmerman was revealed to have been in contact with Mexico, offering aid and assistance if the country would consider invading part of the United States. This, it was hoped by Germany, would keep America busy and stop them thinking about entering the war in Europe.

The projected Mexican attack on the United States was planned to coincide with the resumption by Germany of unrestricted submarine warfare against any ship travelling to or from Britain. This was a calculated gamble, since the Americans had made it clear that they were far from pleased at attacks on their ships in international waters, but the German leaders hoped that it would be possible to break the spirit of the British and bring them to the negotiating table before the United States had time to involve themselves in the war. It was a terrible miscalculation. Just 48 hours after the Germans declared their intention to attack any shipping heading for the British Isles, America broke off diplomatic relations with Germany and then in April declared war. The American perspective was simple. They had, for a century or so, scrupulously avoided involving themselves in European politics, but now a country there was encouraging a neighbour to launch a war on America and was also sinking American ships into the bargain. Retaliating against such hostile actions would be no violation of the Monroe Doctrine, which had never advocated the United States allowing itself to be bullied or harassed by another country, whether in Europe or anywhere else.

Even now though, Wilson eschewed a formal alliance with Britain and France. He said that America would be an 'associate power' and made it clear that although he and his country were opposed to Germany, this by no means meant that they were wholly on the side of Britain. Addressing Congress on 2 April 1917 and setting out the reasons why he wished to take the country to war, Wilson announced that American aims were more lofty than those of Britain, which, he hinted, was more concerned with preserving its empire than it was fighting for justice and right. During the speech, he coined a phrase which was destined to become famous; 'The World must be made safe for democracy'.

The American military contribution to the Allied struggle brought the First World War to a close earlier than most people expected. The enthusiasm in the months following the Armistice was for a new world order, with all nations renouncing war and committed to resolving disputes peacefully. The driving force behind this endeavour, which became the League of Nations, was Woodrow Wilson himself, which makes it all the more ironic that the United States did not ultimately become a member of the new organization, which was a precursor of the United Nations which we know today.

The sticking-point which proved an insurmountable obstacle to the Americans was Article 10 of the League's Covenant. This would commit all signatories 'to respect and preserve as against external aggression the territorial integrity and existing political independence of all Members of the League'.

Such an agreement would of course violate the sacred principle which had become the guiding lodestone of American foreign policy, that the country would be inextricably bound up in an 'entangling alliance' which would oblige them to go to war in Europe or anywhere else where external aggression was being undertaken against another country. The arguments raged in Washington, but it ended in deadlock, with America refusing to join the League of Nations. It also precipitated an upsurge of isolationist sentiment during the decades that followed, which peaked, and then came to an abrupt end, when the Second World War began.

Following the Japanese attack on its naval base at Pearl Harbor in Hawaii on 7 December 1941, the United States had little choice but to declare war on Japan. The following day, Germany and Italy declared war on the United States, which had the effect of ending American isolation and allowing President Roosevelt to join the British in the war against the Nazis without anybody being able to reproach him with having broken the pledges which he had given to American mothers during his election campaign the previous year. Even now though, Roosevelt stopped short of a formal alliance with Britain and the other countries fighting Germany. The United States would certainly do its part in the war, but it would not undertake to defend this or that country or territory. It would formulate its own plans and ultimately it was to be an American general who was in overall charge of the war in Europe.

So it was that America entered the war on Britain's side, but without being bound up with any treaty or agreement.

Chapter 2

Above the Law

It is commonly said in Britain that nobody is above the law. Like all such broad generalizations though, there are exceptions to the rule, the most obvious being in the case of what is known as 'diplomatic immunity'. Since antiquity, heralds and ambassadors have enjoyed special protection and, even if belonging to an enemy nation, may not be molested or harmed. This ancient convention began on the battlefield, when emissaries sent to negotiate a truce or arrange a surrender needed assurances that they would not simply be killed out of hand by the opposing army. As time passed, it became convenient to extend this pledge of safe conduct to permanent representatives of other countries.

In 1709, Britain guaranteed the immunity of foreign diplomatic staff in the country from both civil and criminal legal action. By the twentieth century, most countries abided by similar rules and foreign embassies had come to be recognized as sovereign territory of the country whose government they acted for. It was accepted in all civilized parts of the world that ambassadors and their staff were not answerable to the local law. This was to prevent trumped-up charges being levelled against diplomatic staff as a means of applying pressure on the country which they represented. Exemption from the law of the country where the embassy is situated is absolute. It applies not only to relatively trifling matters such as parking tickets but even armed attacks by embassy staff leading to injury or death. Ambassadors and those working for them in most capacities can quite literally get away with murder. This was neatly demonstrated in Britain in 1984.

On 17 April 1984 a demonstration was held outside the Libyan embassy in London. Two members of the embassy staff opened fire with sub-machine guns, wounding eleven of the demonstrators and killing a young policewoman called Yvonne Fletcher. Eventually, after an armed siege, all thirty of the people in the embassy were allowed to leave, taking with them crates which were marked as diplomatic baggage, which presumably contained the guns used to murder the police officer. Although the police questioned and photographed them all, there was nothing to be done and all were allowed to fly back to Libya.

Of course, diplomatic immunity can be abused and misused. A recent case of this involved the United States and caused something of a scandal in Britain. On 27 August 2019 a 19-year-old man called Harry Dunn was killed in England by a car driving on the wrong side of the road. The death took place near an RAF base which also housed an American listening post. Driving the car was Anne Sacoolas, a former member of the CIA and wife of a man working at the listening station based at RAF Croughton in the English county of Northamptonshire. After the road accident, she was interviewed by the police and claimed diplomatic immunity, through her husband's own status.

When the police in Northamptonshire applied to have Ms Sacoolas' diplomatic immunity revoked, the British Foreign Office informed them that she was not entitled to claim it in the first place. However, it was a moot point, because the Americans had by this time flown her out of the country. This disinclination to allow their citizens to be subject to the law of any other nation has been something of an *idée fixe* with the United States for many years.

The United States has always had a determination, which some say borders on an obsession, to avoid being trapped by treaties and agreements with other nations. In the last chapter we saw that this prevented America from joining the League of Nations after the First World War had ended. More recently, we note that 196 countries, almost every country in the world in fact, has signed up to the United Nations Convention on the Rights of the Child, a legally binding international agreement. The exception is of course the United States. This does not mean that Americans are less concerned about children and their rights than those other countries: it is merely part of their historic horror of binding themselves to treaties drawn up by foreigners. In recent years, this has also led to America's withdrawal from the United Nations Educational, Scientific and Cultural Organization (UNESCO) and the United Nations Human Rights Council (UNHRC) as well. It is even suggested from time to time that the United States might one day leave the United Nations entirely.

A recent instance of this tendency was seen on 6 July 2020, when the United States notified the Secretary General of the United Nations that they would be withdrawing from the World Health Organization in 2021. Every single country belonging to the United Nations, with the exception of Lichtenstein, belongs to the World Health Organization, which was founded in 1948. It is the oldest arm of the United Nations and for America to withdraw from the body was seen by many observers as incomprehensibly reckless. It is only by understanding the background to the American view of foreign policy that it makes any sense.

The United States did not join Britain and France in any formal alliance against Germany in 1941, because of precisely this distaste at becoming confined and constricted by treaties and obligations. This created a slight problem when American troops were due to arrive in the United Kingdom in 1942. The Allied Forces Act 1940 had been passed to allow the governments of Belgium, Czechoslovakia, the Netherlands, Norway and Poland to raise armies and station them on British soil. It was tacitly agreed that they would be allowed to run their own affairs on their military bases and that the British police would not concern themselves unduly about what went on. It was also understood, although not explicitly stated, that this would only apply to their own people and that it would be a different matter if British civilians were to be the victims of crimes committed by foreign troops. This was perfectly reasonable in time of war and the only forces which really sailed close to the wind and pushed the boundaries of what was acceptable were the Poles under the command of General Sikorski.

Poland was a special case as far as Britain was concerned, because after the Fall of France and evacuation of Dunkirk in 1940, they were keen for the 20,000 or so Polish soldiers who were also taken from the French beaches between 26 May and 4 June to aid in the defence of Britain. There was a very real danger that the Germans would launch an invasion of Britain in 1940 and so the Polish army was sent to Scotland to defend that part of the United Kingdom. In return for this assistance, the Polish government in exile was given a free hand to enforce discipline in their army as they saw fit. Under the terms of an Anglo-Polish Military Agreement, the Polish army bases were treated as being sovereign territory, in much the same way as foreign embassies. Some of the Polish camps were used to hold political detainees, men at odds with the government in exile, which was based in London. From time to time, people were killed at such camps and the British police did not investigate, because both the victims and those who killed them were Polish.

On 29 October 1940, a Jewish prisoner called Edward Jakubosky was shot dead at Kingledoors Camp in Scotland. The guard who shot him, Marian Pyzybylski, was not punished for his action. The local police were not involved in the matter at all. Had the victim of the shooting been a British civilian, then things would have been quite different, but as long as foreign soldiers were merely shooting each other or their own compatriots, it was officially felt that nothing needed to be done. There were many ugly rumours circulating in Scotland about what might be going on in the camps for political prisoners, to the extent that the question was raised in Parliament. But as long as it all stayed among the Poles, the government was not minded to ask too many questions. The Polish army was too useful for the defence of that part of the British Isles to run any risk of falling out with Sikorski and his government in exile.

It might have been thought that the United States would have been content to send their troops to Britain under similarly lax conditions, allowing them to do pretty much as they pleased within the confines of their own bases, but President Roosevelt demanded, and ultimately got, far more than this. He wanted an assurance that whatever any American soldier did, that man would be completely beyond the reach of British law. This immunity from prosecution was to be absolute and unconditional, for any kind of offence, up to and including murder. Every single member of the United States armed forces in Britain would be free of any risk of arrest by the police for anything at all that he did. Such criminals would be answerable only to American law and American justice, administered by Americans.

Set out as plainly as this, it is hard to imagine any country agreeing to invite an army onto its soil over which it would have no control and whose soldiers were completely free from any of the laws which applied to everybody else. Certainly, had a Polish or French soldier murdered or raped a civilian, then the machinery of justice would have been brought into play without reference to anybody. Only the peculiar circumstances of those desperate times can explain why the British agreed to such demands from the United States government. The truth is that without American military assistance, there was not the remotest chance of Britain being able to defeat Germany. The best that could be hoped for was for Britain to remain an independent nation, on the fringe of a continent ruled by the Nazis, a prospect which was unthinkable. It was for this reason that the British government, albeit with considerable misgivings, accepted the American proposals in their entirety. On 27 July 1942 Anthony Eden, who was then at the Foreign Office and who later of course became Prime Minister, wrote to the American ambassador and outlined the proposals which had been discussed. After sketching out what had been said so far, he said;

In view of the very considerable departure which the above arrangements will involve from the traditional system and practice of the United Kingdom there are certain points upon which His Majesty's Government considers it indispensable first to reach an understanding with the United States Government.

After reminding the ambassador that he had agreed that any American soldier who committed a crime in Britain would be dealt with by court martial, Eden continued;

> His Majesty's Government will be glad if Your Excellency will confirm their understanding that the trial of any member of the United States Forces for an offence against the civilian population would be in open court (except where security considerations forbade this) and would be arranged to take place promptly in the United Kingdom and within a reasonable distance from the spot where the offence was alleged to have been committed, so that witnesses should not be required to travel great distances to attend the hearing.

The American ambassador was a little vague about some of the assurances which the British requested and when the United States of America (Visiting Forces) Act 1942 was passed by Parliament that August, none of what Eden had been so anxious about found its way into the legislation, which simply stated that 'no criminal proceedings shall be prosecuted in the United Kingdom before any court against a member of the military or naval forces of the United States'. The British government simply had to trust the Americans to follow the spirit, and not merely the letter, of the law.

The wording of the United States of America (Visiting Forces) Act differed sharply from the provisions of the Allied Forces Act, which had been passed two years earlier and applied to the armies of the various European countries which were based in the United Kingdom. That earlier act was very clear that:

> Nothing . . . shall affect the jurisdiction of any civil court in the United Kingdom, or of any colony or territory to which that section is extended, to try a member of any of the naval, military or air forces mentioned in that section for any act or

omission constituting an offence against the law of the United Kingdom, or of that colony or territory, as the case may be.

There was nothing here about immunity from prosecution, quite the opposite in fact. Although the authorities might have turned a blind eye to activities within the various armies, this was by way of a favour. Legally, every Polish, French, Dutch and Norwegian soldier in Britain was as strictly bound by the law as any British citizen.

In the event, the US Army was scrupulous about ensuring that no soldier would remain unpunished for any offence against civilians in Britain. The reason that the ambassador did not wish to have all this enshrined in law was not because America was intending to allow its troops to get away with robbery, rape or murder. It was simply that same historic dread at which we have looked already, of being bound up in some treaty which would oblige them to follow the wishes of a foreign power, rather than having a free hand. In the event, it was the British who wanted some of the proceedings against US servicemen convicted of brutal crimes to take place not only not 'within a reasonable distance from the spot where the offence was alleged to have been committed' but on the other side of the Atlantic Ocean. Specifically, there was unease about the idea of executions being carried out in the United Kingdom following American courts martial.

Frank Newsam was the second highest-ranking civil servant at the Home Office and it was he who had chiefly been responsible for negotiating the legal position of US soldiers with the Americans. It was these discussions which would eventually shape the relevant piece of legislation. Although he wanted the trials or courts martial to take place near to the location where the supposed crimes had been committed, Newsam did not care at all for the idea of executions taking place on British soil of men who had not been tried by British courts, something which most of those involved in discussing the matter regarded as very likely to happen. He wrote to a colleague that, 'We should take up with the Americans the question of the desirability of carrying out these sentences in America'. This was done, but on the American side there was stiff opposition to the idea of shipping a condemned criminal back to the United States and executing him there. Colonel Edward Betts, the Judge Advocate General, did not agree at all that this would be a good idea. He did not think that the US authorities would want this because, 'if a man was taken away to be executed his fellow soldiers would not believe the sentence had been carried out and the deterrent effect would be lessened'. Colonel Betts almost certainly had in mind the kind of cases which did actually occur when once American forces had arrived in Britain.

On 27 December 1942, a young soldier called David Cobb shot an officer dead after being reprimanded. It was thought important that an example should be made of him, to deter any other young conscripts who might be minded to start shooting their officers. Although it was open to the court martial to impose either the death penalty or imprisonment for life, they felt that this was such a serious breach of discipline that a severe example should be made of Cobb, who became the first American soldier to be executed in England. The effect of his execution would have been greatly lessened had he been transported across the Atlantic and hanged in an American prison. As it was, it was widely publicized that he had been hanged at Shepton Mallet and this was no doubt noted by any other men who might have been feeling rebellious. This then was the reason that the Judge Advocate General wished for such sentences to be carried out expeditiously and in the same country in which the crime had been committed.

How necessary were all these high-level talks about the hypothetical case of soldiers possibly committing this crime or that? Was it not a pessimistic approach to the matter, assuming almost as a matter of course that some of those American servicemen would cross the ocean and then start killing, stealing and raping? Unfortunately, history teaches us that soldiers in wartime do tend to run wild, as though all the normal rules of civilized conduct no longer apply. This is especially the case when they are far from their own country. There was no reason to suppose that the US Army would deviate from this general trend. The statistics of crime in Britain during the Second World War confirm that it was wise to decide how to deal with a possible crime wave before, rather than after, it began.

In the three years or so between their arrival in Britain in 1942 and the end of the war in 1945, American soldiers killed no fewer than fifty-three people, none of whom were enemy soldiers. Of these deaths, twenty-six resulted in convictions for murder and the others were categorized as manslaughter. In addition to this, 126 rapes were committed by members of the US forces in Britain over the same period. Clearly, those who had been trying to work out how to deal with such things had been right to plan ahead.

Having agreed in principle that American soldiers would not be held by the British police or tried in British courts, the obvious question was how they would in fact be dealt with, that is to say, who would try them when they were accused of some crime and if they were to be imprisoned or executed, how would this work, if the British judicial system was not to be involved at any stage. These questions proved fairly easy to answer, but in the process raised another which was to prove rather more difficult to tackle.

The US forces stationed in the United Kingdom would be governed by military law, specifically the Articles of War which had been approved on 4 June 1920. These listed, in addition to such purely military offences as mutiny and desertion, all the commonest of ordinary crimes. Article 93, entitled Various Crimes, read as follows;

> Any person subject to military law who commits manslaughter, mayhem, arson, burglary, housebreaking, robbery, larceny, embezzlement, perjury, forgery, sodomy, assault with intent to commit any felony, assault with intent to do bodily harm with a dangerous weapon, instrument, or other thing, or assault with intent to do bodily harm, shall be punished as a court-martial may direct.

This seemed to both the British and Americans to cover most of the usual things which unruly soldiers might get up to during the chaos of war.

Agreement having been reached on the question of who would proceed against soldiers accused of any of the above offences, that they would be dealt with by court martial, the next question was how they were to be punished. If sentenced to prison, then would they serve their time in a British establishment or be sent back to the United States? Since, as we have seen, the American legal authorities were not keen on shipping convicted prisoners back across the Atlantic, this was something which would have to be decided fairly soon.

When all the different factors had been considered and weighed up, the solution was simplicity itself. The British Army had taken over an empty and all but derelict prison at the outbreak of war in 1939. It was in an out-of-the-way location in the West Country and could be handed over to the US Army as it was. They could then operate it as their very own military prison. Executions had been conducted at this particular prison and although the gallows and execution shed were in poor shape, they could easily be rebuilt. So it was that the oldest purpose-built prison in Britain was cleared of British troops and the keys made ready to hand over to the US Army when they began arriving in 1942.

Chapter 3

The Oldest Prison in England

Today, the most severe judicial punishment which anybody might suffer in Britain is imprisonment. We are so familiar with the concept of deprivation of one's liberty as the worst penalty which the law can inflict, that it comes as a surprise to discover that prisons are relative newcomers in the field of penology. It is only in the last two or three centuries that the idea of locking people up might be sufficient punishment in itself, without any of the extras such as whipping, branding, torture, starvation or mutilation which often accompanied the practice until well into the twentieth century. In Britain, criminals in prison were still being flogged and their diet restricted to bread and water as late as the 1960s. In Europe today, punishment is limited only to imprisonment, without any additional suffering.

For almost the whole of recorded history, legal penalties have been ferocious and designed to discourage people from crime by demonstrating the horrors which awaited them if they should be found breaking the law. For this reason executions, floggings and so on all took place in public. There would be, according to this way of thinking, little point in punishing a person if the procedure could not be seen by others. There would be no deterrent effect. People might be locked up until their trial, to prevent them from running away, or while they were awaiting execution, say, but keeping a man or woman at the public expense and providing them with free board and lodging would have seemed a very strange idea until as late as the seventeenth or eighteenth century.

The invention of prisons happened almost by accident and that in the Somerset town of Shepton Mallet, which was later to become an American military detention facility, was one of the first to be built.

It, and other similar establishments, appeared following the passing of the Elizabethan Poor Law in 1601. This obliged towns to set up what were called 'Houses of Correction'. Similar in many ways to the workhouses of the nineteenth century, the house of correction was intended as a place where beggars and vagrants would be housed and provided with useful work to do. The sight of wandering vagabonds was offensive to respectable people of the time and they felt that detaining them in a building where they would have to work hard might at least mean that they would not clutter up the streets and create a disorderly atmosphere.

There was what we would today term a moral panic in England during the later sixteenth century, which concerned the supposedly large numbers of what were then known as 'masterless men'. The masterless men were those without work and who owed allegiance to no city or town. They roamed the country, begging, scrounging and, it was widely suspected, stealing. They were sometimes viewed in the same unfavourable light as Gypsies and it was though better from the perspective of social order if they could be detained and compelled to work for their bread like everybody else in Tudor society.

It was only a short step from locking up beggars for a week or two to doing the same with prostitutes, card sharps and petty thieves. Often, the few weeks spent in the house of correction, or Bridewell, as they were also known after a famous one in London, was preceded by a whipping. So it was that by the end of the seventeenth century the idea had taken root that some crimes were best dealt with by locking people up for a spell. This is the origin of the current practice of depriving people of their liberty and considering this to be a punishment in itself, without the addition of whipping or branding.

Very little money was available for the maintenance of the Bridewells and most fell into disrepair, although they still had many inmates. Wherever possible, towns and cities hoped to make these places self-supporting financially. This was done by providing the most meagre fare imaginable, which meant that the prisoners wished to buy food and liquor to supplement their diet. The jailers thus made a profit from this, as well as by buying other goods from outside and selling them to the inmates, always retaining a certain percentage of the money for themselves. The jailers at Shepton Mallet were not paid and so there was every incentive for them to engage in such practices. It was their only source of income. For the same reasons of economy, the Shepton Mallet House of Correction was not kept in good order and no repairs were carried out for the first 30 years after it was built. By the time of the English Civil War, it was said to be in a very poor state. Illustration 2 shows an old section of the wall at Shepton Mallet Prison, consisting of roughly-hewn blocks of limestone. It is a solid, rather than aesthetically pleasing, style of building.

Over a century later, in 1773, the prison at Shepton Mallet was in an even worse condition than it had been in the middle of the seventeenth century. John Howard, whose name is still familiar to us today from the Howard League for Penal Reform, had been appointed by Parliament to investigate the state of the country's prisons. What he found at Shepton Mallet shocked him. He wrote that;

> Many who went in healthy are in a few months changed to emaciated, dejected objects. Some are seen pining under diseases, expiring on the floors, in loathsome cells, of pestilential fevers, and the confluent smallpox. Victims, I will not say to cruelty, but I must say to the inattention of the Sheriffs, and Gentlemen in the commission of peace. The cause of this distress is, that many prisons are scantily supplied, and some almost totally unprovided with the necessaries of life.

At the time that Howard visited Shepton Mallet, men and women were not housed separately. Sometimes, visitors were smuggled in by jailers; wives or prostitutes were allowed to spend the night. However, a shakeup of British prisons was on the way. Many of the old abuses were to be done away with and as imprisonment was becoming an increasingly common punishment, it was felt that it was time to put prisons on a more businesslike and less haphazard footing.

Part of the reluctance to invest any substantial sums of money in the creation of or maintenance of prisons was that a simpler and cheaper alternative existed for taking incorrigible criminals out of circulation and keeping them away from respectable folk. This was of course the system of transportation. Until the 1770s and the American Revolution, it was possible to ship convicted thieves and other criminals off to America, where they became somebody else's problem. Just at the time that people like John Howard were investigating, and complaining about, the conditions in British prisons, this option of sending undesirables to America ended. Of course, soon afterwards Australia became a new dumping-ground and in 1787 the first ship containing convicts sailed for Botany Bay. The end of transportation to America though prompted a general reappraisal of what to do with those who broke the law and an expansion of prisons was one natural consequence.

From the early nineteenth century onwards, those confined in Shepton Mallet Prison, as it now was, would be expected to work hard. It was thought that having the men lolling about all day long had a bad effect on them both morally and spiritually and provision was made for them to be kept fully occupied. A life of hard work was felt to be more conducive to reformation than idleness. Boulders were brought into the prison for the men to break down into small pieces with hammers, so that these could be used for building roads. Others were set to work pulling apart old tarred ropes, turning them into caulking for the wooden ships of the time. This activity, also imposed upon the inmates of workhouses, became a byword for dull and demeaning labour. In 1823 a treadmill was installed in the prison. This was an enormous wheel, something like the paddle wheel of an old steamship, on which forty men at a time would work. It was like an endless staircase and for hours at a time the prisoners would operate this fearsome machine, which ran a grain mill outside the prison walls. After a day spent on the treadmill, few men had any energy left for rioting or other violence.

There were two other prisons in Somerset, one in Taunton and the other in Ilchester. By 1845, Ilchester had closed and Shepton Mallet was holding around 250 prisoners. It was not long after this that the decision was made to build a set of gallows at Shepton Mallet. Because it is so long since anybody in Britain has been hanged, it is easy to forget how common executions once were. Even small provincial prisons such as St Albans and Bedford had gallows in them. Executions were never especially common at Shepton Mallet, which was perhaps why, when the Americans took over in 1942, they were obliged to build a new execution chamber. The existing gallows was too old to be able to rely upon it and an entirely new structure had to be built.

Between 1889 and 1926, just seven people were hanged on the Shepton Mallet gallows. All were executed for unremarkable murders, although the last hanging which took place at the prison is notable for three reasons. These are the executioner who carried it out, the father of the condemned man and the fact that the Home Secretary was questioned in Parliament about the circumstances under which the hanging took place.

What became known at the time as the Trowbridge Murder took place in the Wiltshire town of that name on Christmas Eve 1925. A well-to-do businessman called Edward Richards was shot dead in the back garden of his home in Victoria Avenue, Trowbridge. He had been hit by no fewer than seven bullets and it was not difficult to find either the motive for the crime, nor the man who had committed it. At the time of his death, Edward Richards had over £40 in cash on him, a considerable sum of money a century ago, and also various cheques and bonds. This looked very much like a bungled robbery and two soldiers from the nearby Trowbridge Barracks were arrested the following day. One of these men rejoiced in the improbably exotic name of Ignatius Emanuel Naphtali Trebich Lincoln, known as 'John' for short. Both he and his companion were charged with murder, although the other man was acquitted of this charge when the case came to trial.

There was considerable interest in the arrest of John Lincoln, because his father was a very colourful character who had at different times been a priest in the Church of England, Member of Parliament for the northern constituency of Darlington, spy, financier and jailed confidence trickster. That this well-known character's son was accused of murder made national headlines. Perhaps inevitably, in view of the fact that he had, rather imprudently, confessed to the crime in a letter to his sweetheart sent while he was on remand, Lincoln was convicted and sentenced to death. Public interest remained high in John Lincoln after he had been lodged in the condemned cell and was even higher after his execution, for reasons we shall look at.

John Lincoln's father, Trebitsch Lincoln, had been born in Hungary and later acquired British citizenship. Following his trial and imprisonment for fraud during the First World War, the government had deported him and revoked his citizenship. At the time of his son's trial, he was in South America, but had expressed the desire to see his son for one last time before he was hanged. Newspapers played up the human-interest angle of this story for all that they were worth, speculating as to whether Trebitsch Lincoln would make it back to Britain before the execution took place. In the event, he did not, but it certainly sold a lot of newspapers.

John Lincoln was hanged at 8:00 am on 2 March 1926 by Tom Pierrepoint, the man who would hang most of the Americans who were executed at Shepton Mallet during the Second World War. Almost immediately, a rumour began to circulate that the crowd in a street near the prison had actually heard the sound of the drop falling during Lincoln's execution. We cannot know at this late stage if there was anything in this story or, as seems more likely, it was just something invented by newspaper reporters to ring the last few drops out of the Trowbridge Murder, but the matter was eventually raised in Parliament.

On 11 March 1926 Colonel Harry Day, the MP for London's Southwark district, rose to ask the Home Secretary,

> If his attention has been drawn to the fact that the execution shed at Shepton Mallet Gaol is against the wall of the prison, and that at the execution on the 2nd March a large crowd of men, women, and children were able, by placing their ears to the said wall, to hear the execution; and will he take steps to prevent a repetition of this?

Home Secretary Sir William Joynson-Hicks was annoyed at hearing this awful tale being raised in the House and he was quite curt and dismissive in his reply to Colonel Day;

> The execution was carried out, not in a shed against the outer wall of the prison, but in a brick building 43 feet from that wall. It is difficult to believe that persons behaving in the manner described could have heard what is suggested.

This is interesting because when the US Army took over the prison, they set up a precisely similar system, in a brick building which was virtually identical to the one which had been used up to 1926.

Four and a half years after the final civilian execution at Shepton Mallet, the prison closed. There were by that time only fifty-one inmates and it was uneconomic to keep running such a large prison containing so few prisoners. From September 1930 until the outbreak of war in 1939, Shepton Mallet Prison remained empty, apart from a caretaker to keep an eye on the property.

When the Second World War began for Britain in the summer of 1939, the armed forces took over Shepton Mallet Prison. It was also used for the storage of important historical documents which were removed from London in case they should be destroyed in air raids. These included the Domesday Book and the log of Nelson's flagship

HMS *Victory.* Most of these remained there until the end of the war in 1945. Scholars and researchers were still able to access these papers and books, but instead of visiting the Public Record Office in London, they were obliged to travel to an out-of-the-way corner of the West Country.

It was in 1942 that Shepton Mallet became an exclusively American detention facility. It had been guessed from the start that some soldiers were likely to misbehave when they were far from their homes and that there would be a need for somewhere to lock them up. It was also a reasonable assumption that a certain number would commit crimes which merited the death penalty and so a set of gallows would also be required. Even before the first American soldiers landed in Britain, the decision had already been taken that they would have to follow British practice if executions were to take place.

The gallows on which Tom Pierrepoint had hanged John Lincoln was in a poor state and rather than repair it, it was thought better to build an entirely new execution chamber and gallows. It had to be constructed to Home Office specifications so that any hangings were conducted as painlessly as possible. Some of the details of the gallows were unique to the British way of hanging and it is unlikely that anybody building a set of gallows would have thought of including them, unless they were familiar with the British way of undertaking executions. To give one example, there was provision for preventing the trapdoors from recoiling after they had been released. In a later chapter we shall be looking at the way that the executions of high-ranking Nazis were conducted by a US Army hangman in 1946, after the Nuremberg trials.

When the bodies of the hanged Nazi leaders, the politicians and generals who had led the Third Reich and been responsible for so many war crimes, were displayed after they had been hanged, it was very noticeable that some of their faces were covered in blood. There was a very simple explanation for this. When the trapdoor of the gallows gives way, the condemned man of course plunges down, until the rope around his neck brings the victim to a sudden halt. The heavy wooden doors though typically bang against the framework of the gallows and rebound, causing them to fly back into the path of the falling body. When this happens, they can both act to slow the descent slightly, making a broken neck less likely, but it is also possible that they will strike the person's face or head, causing injuries. This is what happened at Nuremberg, most notably to Field Marshal Wilhelm Keitel. The British avoided this problem by having spring catches which caught the trapdoors after they had fallen, holding them tight and preventing them from flapping about. The steel springs were covered in rubber, to reduce the noise. Nobody wanted the booming of the operation of the gallows to echo around a prison.

The Americans made no objection to any of this. It mattered little to them what modifications the British made to the process of hanging, nor even if the man putting the rope around the murderer or rapist's neck was British or American. As long as they were the sole arbiters of innocence or guilt and their men were immune from the law of the land, they were happy.

The US Army undertook the building of the new execution chamber and gallows in 1942, when Shepton Mallet Prison was handed over to them. They used ordinary bricks, which contrasted with the old stone of which the rest of the prison was built. It was a brutally functional building, which was simply tacked on to an existing wing of the prison. The two-storey structure consisted of a room with a beam running across the ceiling. This was the gallows. Beneath it was a trapdoor. On the ground floor was a stone mortuary slab, where the body of the executed man would be laid once he had been taken down from the gallows. The drop from the execution chamber was this room. Illustration 8 shows this new building. When seen against the white stone of the original prison buildings, shown in Illustration 1, the red bricks used for this ugly structure really do stand out.

In Illustration 9, the inside of the execution chamber may be seen. There is no sign now of the beam of the gallows, which used to run along the ceiling. After the end of the war, the gallows was dismantled and floorboards laid over the space where once there was a trapdoor.

This room became the prison library. Shepton Mallet Prison is at the time of writing open as a museum and some of the floorboards in the execution chamber have been removed to indicate where the trapdoor would have been. This is the area surrounded by rails in Illustration 9. When the boards were removed, it was found that the marks where the hinges of the trapdoors had been were still plainly visible in the rafters below. These may be seen in Illustration 10.

To begin with the prison was designated by the US Army as the 6833rd Guardhouse Overhead Detachment. Later, this was changed and it was known for the rest of the war as The Headquarters 2912th Disciplinary Training Center – APO 508 United States Army. The first commandant of this new establishment was Lieutenant Colonel James P. Smith of the 707th Military Police Battalion. It swiftly became apparent that there was a great need for a purely American military prison. The number of prisoners rose steadily over the next two years and by late 1944, no fewer than 768 men were held at Shepton Mallet. Guarding the prison were twelve officers, commanding eighty-two enlisted men.

It is time now to try and see why the British were so adamant that their own technique for hanging should be used and not that commonly employed in the United States. At first sight, it seems a little strange to make such a fuss about whose hangman should have the job of despatching a criminal. As we shall see in the next chapter, this was not so much a matter of British national pride as an honest desire that any man being executed in their country should suffer as little pain as possible. Since this apparently minor point caused the British to dig in their heels so firmly and refuse to give an inch in negotiations, it was clearly of great importance, at least from the British side. We need to look now at how Britain executed murderers and how its methods of hanging differed from those of every other country in the world.

Chapter 4

The Mechanics of Hanging

We come now to what, on the face of it, is a very puzzling matter. As we have seen, the British government was content to allow every single member of the American armed forces to be above and beyond the law of the land. No policeman could touch them, nor any British court claim jurisdiction over them. More than that, the US Army in Britain had been given a prison, complete with gallows, so that they could lock up or execute any of their men they chose. The only point on which the British were utterly immovable was that no American executioner was to be allowed to hang anybody. Any hangings could only be conducted by one of the men provided by the Home Office for that purpose. To understand this curious obduracy on the part of the British government, it will be necessary to make a detour into the history of hanging.

Hanging is one of the most ancient methods of judicial execution. It is mentioned both in the Bible, in the Book of Esther, with the hanging of Haman on the gallows which he had caused to be built for his enemy Mordechai, and also in Homer's *Odyssey*. Book XXII of the *Odyssey*, written in the eighth century BC, tells how Odysseus' son Telemachus hanged some disloyal female servants. Traditional hanging has the great advantage of being exceedingly simple to carry out and requiring no particular skill on the part of the executioner. This is in contrast to methods such as the use of firearms, which needs a degree of proficiency if it is to be carried out cleanly and expeditiously. Suspending a person by means of a ligature around the neck will result in death, with no fuss, lengthy preparations or specialized equipment. In its simplest form, only a rope and tree are necessary. Leave somebody hanging in that way by his or her neck and death will, given enough time, inevitably ensue.

The early method of hanging, used for 3,000 years or so, typically caused death by asphyxiation. The pressure of the rope around the neck blocked the windpipe and the victim simply choked to death. It may have been a sure means of bringing about death, but it was often a painful and distressing one, with those executed in this way struggling for breath, kicking their legs and usually losing control of their bladders as they died. It was a degrading and humiliating end, but that was really the point. Hanging has always been seen as an undignified mode of execution, reserved for common criminals. Beheading or shooting were both seen as being far better and more honourable ways to die.

The physical agony suffered by those being hanged, along with features like the uncontrollable voiding of urine in the final extremity, were regarded as good things by those in authority. Until the late eighteenth century and the dawning of the Age of Reason, the whole point of executions was that they should be as frightful as possible. It was believed at this time that the more terrible the death endured by convicted criminals, the more care people would take to avoid suffering in the same way. Pain and degradation during the course of an execution were felt to be wholesome for the general population to witness and likely to keep them on the straight and narrow. This is of course why elaborate and protracted methods of execution were devised, such as breaking on the wheel or hanging, drawing and quartering. The sight of a man being castrated and disembowelled while conscious was thought to be a wholesome one for anybody in the watching crowd who might have it in mind in the future to commit treason.

Not all those hanged by the neck underwent a protracted death by strangulation. Sometimes, the condemned person's neck was broken and this meant an instantaneous and almost painless end. Guy Fawkes, for example, was the most famous conspirator in what became known as the Gunpowder Plot, a plan to assassinate King James I and his entire government. The men responsible for this attempted mass murder were sentenced to be hanged, drawn and quartered. This entailed hanging them briefly and then, while they were still conscious, castrating and disembowelling them. It was the worst punishment available to the courts at that time.

When Guy Fawkes was hanged, a common way of going about it was to make the condemned man climb a ladder, with the hangman coming up behind him. The noose was then placed around his neck and he was pushed off, to dangle and choke. Anxious to avoid the tortures which awaited him after being suspended for a few seconds, Fawkes leaped from the ladder and the fall was so violent that his neck was broken. He was spared the horrors of castration and the rest of the grisly process.

For the next few centuries, the technique used for executions in Britain did not change much. Sometimes a ladder was used, at others the prisoners were placed on a cart, the rope tied around their necks and the cart pulled away. In almost every case, death was by slow strangulation. From time to time, there were those like Guy Fawkes who jumped into space, hoping for a swifter and less agonizing death. With the coming of the Industrial Revolution, the old methods used for hanging began to seem a little outdated. Machinery was being used for all sorts of things at the beginning of the nineteenth century, replacing the slow old ways of craftsmanship by hand. Instead of a ladder or horse and cart, gallows with mechanical drops were constructed. Apart from a desire to be more modern, it was thought that this might prove to be a humane way to despatch those due to die. By the time of the Napoleonic Wars, the idea that the spectacle of public executions should be as cruel as possible was declining. The aim now was to end the lives of convicted criminals with as little suffering as possible. The important point being that they died for their crimes, rather than being forced to suffer first.

The new 'short drop' gallows which appeared in various British cities at this time consisted of a platform upon which the condemned men and women stood. The rope fixed round their necks had a little slack, typically 2ft or so. When the platform fell, the prisoner dropped for a short distance, before being jerked up short by the noose. Sometimes, this happened to snap the neck, but more often than not it simply shocked the hanged person into momentary immobility; he or she then choked to death as in the earlier type of execution. Because they had been stunned, the struggles were often feebler and less vigorous. It *looked* as though the victim was suffering less. The whole arrangement was rather like a stage, the lower half of the hanging person being hidden from view and so the executioner was able to go below and hang on the legs of anybody who was struggling too violently and giving the impression to the watching crowds that the death had been painless and quick. This is of course the origin of the expression to pull somebody's leg, meaning a sham or imposture.

In 1862 an obscure and little-known journal called *The London, Edinburgh and Dublin Philosophical Magazine* carried an article by an Irish doctor called Samuel Haughton. Executions were at that time carried out in public and Dr Haughton had been horrified to witness a hanging which used the 'short drop' method. The victim had died painfully, choking to death, rather than having his neck cleanly broken. After giving the matter considerable though, Haughton wrote a piece called, 'On hanging, considered from a mechanical and physiological point of view'. His opinion as a medical man was that it ought to be possible to calculate how far to drop a person being executed in order to ensure that the neck was broken at once. Haughton believed that a force of something over 2,000 foot-pounds would be needed to ensure that the neck snapped.

Samuel Haughton's article prompted a change in the way that men and women were hanged, not only in Ireland, but also the rest of Britain and as far away as the United States. In Britain, hanging became more or less an art, with both the machinery of the gallows and length of the drop being refined until death was inflicted instantaneously every time. America adopted part of the new method, but development there stalled, which was why of course when the US Army sentenced men to be hanged during the Second World War, the British government insisted that their own executioners should carry out the sentences.

An early instance of the United States' use of the 'long drop' may be seen in the execution of the three men and one woman who were convicted of involvement in the assassination of Abraham Lincoln in 1865. The man who actually fired the lethal shot, John Wilkes Booth, died in a gun battle 12 days after killing the president. A number of other people thought to have aided Booth and colluded in his plans were brought before a military court, following which they were sentenced to death. The hangings took place on 7 July 1865, almost three months after Lincoln's death. Although by that time the United States had widely adopted the 'long drop', not one of those hanged that day died of a broken neck. All four choked to death and their execution provides a textbook example of how not to conduct a hanging neatly, humanely and expeditiously. Since the methods used that day remained unchanged over the next century, we may examine this execution to see why the British government were adamant that no American-style hangings would be taking place in their own country.

Illustration 3 shows us all we need to know about the American way of hanging. We see a woman, Mary Surrat, hanging at the end of a rope next to Lewis Payne, another of the conspirators hanged for being mixed up in Lincoln's assassination. It will be seen at once that although the woman is much shorter than the man, their heads are level with each other when hanging side by side. This tells us that a fixed drop was given of about 6ft. No adjustment was made in the length of the drop to ensure that both necks received the same amount of force when they were jerked to a halt after falling. Obviously, the lighter Mary Surrat's neck would have been subjected to less stress than that of Lewis Payne's. All four executed people that day received the same standard drop. On the other hand, in the second half of the nineteenth century the British drew up a series of tables, carefully calculating how far a person of any weight should be allowed to fall in order to generate a force to their neck of around 1,000 foot-pounds, about half of what Samuel Haughton believed necessary. This then is the first feature of

American hangings which made the process unreliable. Until as late as the 1960s, a fixed drop was the practice.

Looking again at Illustration 3 we see that the ropes have ended up at the back of the two victims' necks. This was the opposite of the British method, where the rope, when taut, would be at the front of the neck, throwing the head far enough back to break the neck. A rope which ended up at the back of the neck was not able to force the chin back, effectively levering apart the vertebrae and ensuring instant loss of consciousness and death. The ideal aimed at during judicial hanging of this kind is the separation of the second and third or fourth and fifth cervical vertebra, the so-called 'hangman's fracture'. This may be seen in Illustration 4. To achieve this end, it is vital that the knot is placed beneath the left ear, so that when it tightens at the end of the drop, the knot ends up beneath the chin.

The third feature of the execution seen in Illustration 3 is one which was still seen in American hangings as late as the 1990s, when the last executions of this kind took place in the United States. Just visible at the back of Mary Surrat's neck is a dark rectangle. This is the classic 'cowboy coil' hangman's noose which was largely developed in America and invariably used for judicial hanging. This type of noose alone makes a clean death from the breaking of the neck unlikely, for the following reason. It is not the drop, as such, which breaks the neck during a judicial hanging. It is rather the rapidity with which the knot around the neck tightens, combined with the position in which it ended up. For this reason, it is essential that the noose is able to tighten freely. An example of the traditional, 'cowboy coil' noose may be seen in Illustration 5.

When the 'long drop' first began to be used in Britain, it was realized that the sort of slipknot then commonly seen at executions would not do at all. Something far looser and more easily able to pull tight would be needed. For this enormous improvement in the technique of judicial hanging, we are indebted to a shoemaker from Lincolnshire. At the age of 52, William Marwood decided that he would be far better at hanging people humanely than the then chief hangman, a man called William Calcraft. Calcraft, in his seventies at that time, had been the hangman for over 40 years and his executions were famous for being brutal affairs in which the victims choked to death slowly. This was because he used a short drop of 3–4ft and gave no thought to where the knot was placed.

William Marwood pestered the governor of Lincoln Prison to allow him the opportunity of demonstrating his new method of hanging and, incredible as it might seem, in 1872 he was engaged to hang a man convicted of murder. His method proved to be far more expeditious than that used by the aging Calcraft and within 18 months, Calcraft had been pensioned off and Marwood appointed chief executioner in his place. Perhaps the most radical improvement in the process devised by Marwood was the new kind of noose which he designed and had made to his specifications. An example of this, the noose used in all British executions from the 1870s right up to the abolition of hanging in Britain in the 1960s, may be seen in Illustration 6.

Anybody who has actually made a 'cowboy coil' noose from thick hemp rope will know that pulling it tight is very hard. This is because of the friction inherent in such a knot. In the noose invented by William Marwood though, there is practically no friction at all to impede the tightening. The rope simply runs freely through the metal ring woven into the end of the rope. Once the victim reached the end of the rope, after falling 6 or 8ft, this type of noose would simply snap the neck like a matchstick. Combined with the table of recommended drops drawn up by Marwood, it meant that instantaneous death was practically guaranteed every time.

One final aspect of hanging as it was practised in Britain needs to be mentioned and this was the judgement of the hangman himself. Even with a table of drops, the kind of thing seen in Illustration 7, adjustments needed to be made for age, gender and physique. A healthy and physically active 20-year-old man would generally have stronger neck muscles than a woman of 50 and this too would need to be borne in mind. If too long a drop were given to somebody with feeble muscles in his or her neck, then the results could be ghastly. It was such a case in the United States which influenced the British decision not to allow the US Army to carry out hangings.

The fixed-drop hangings which were favoured in the United States, together with the use of the classic 'cowboy coil' noose and indifference to the position around the neck when placing of the knot, meant that executions by this means in the United States were very much a hit-and-miss business, with many of the victims dying of strangulation rather than broken necks. This was bad, but there could be a much worse outcome if attention was not paid to the physical condition of the condemned prisoner. A widely publicized incident during an execution just 12 years before the arrival of US forces in Britain gives us a good example of just how woefully deficient American methods could be when it came to hanging people. It is entirely possible that it was the details of this appalling business which hardened the hearts of the British government against allowing the Americans to organize any hangings in the United Kingdom.

In 1927 a 49-year-old woman called Eva Dugan murdered the man who had employed her as a housekeeper and went on the run. By the time she was brought to trial, some months later, it had been discovered that the dumpy middle-aged widow had been married five times, but all her husbands had vanished without trace. Whether this prejudiced the authorities against her, it is hard to say, but she was charged with her former employer's murder and convicted. Since gaining statehood no woman had been hanged in Arizona, which meant that the forthcoming execution generated a good deal of interest.

The execution of Eva Dugan took place at a few minutes after 5:00 am on 21 February 1930. This was a time when hangings in America were changing from being public spectacles to private affairs conducted within the walls of a prison. But although this execution was nominally private, well over fifty witnesses had been invited into the Arizona State Prison in Florence for the event. Among them were many newspaper reporters, which made what happened impossible to hush up. A number of women were also among the witnesses.

For a British hangman, the fact that the condemned person was a middle-aged woman whose neck was distinctly flabby would have been a sign that a reduced drop was called for. As it was that day, a fixed drop was used, with no regard to either the weight or physical condition of the prisoner. This revealed in the starkest way imaginable the shortcomings of the system as it was then being practised.

Eva Dugan showed no fear as she was escorted up the steps of the gallows, which was erected in a building somewhat like a warehouse. The watching crowd saw her walk to the centre of the trapdoor, where the rope was placed around her neck. Once everything was ready the executioner pulled the lever, sending the 52-year-old woman hurtling down, until stopped abruptly by the rope around her neck. A contemporary newspaper report relates what happened at that point. According to the *LA Times*, 'When the trap was sprung the first impact of the knotted rope snapped Mrs. Dugan's head from her body.' As if this was not horrible enough, the decapitated head bounced from the gallows and landed at the feet of the nearest witnesses, at which point three men and two women fainted.

What had happened, of course, was that the muscles of Eva Dugan's neck had been so weak that when the jerk at the end of the rope snapped the bones, it also tore apart the muscles, meaning that there was no longer anything attaching the head to the trunk. The gruesome circumstances of the execution were soon being reported around the world. A song was even composed about the event and released as a gramophone record. The ballad *The Hanging of Eva Dugan* began by referring to the fact that she was the first woman legally hanged in Arizona; 'Down in Arizona was just the other day, The first time that a woman the death price had to pay.'

It was impossible that those making the arrangements associated with the United States of America (Visiting Forces) Act 1942 could have failed to be aware of such mishaps as occurred at the hanging at which we have just looked. They would certainly know too about the unsavoury circumstances surrounding America's last public execution in 1936, when the executioner was too drunk to carry out his duties and a deputy sheriff had to step in and operate the gallows. None of this gave a very favourable impression of American expertise in the field of hanging and contributed to the determination of the British that if anybody was to be hanged in their country, then the job would be undertaken by properly trained professionals.

Chapter 5

Execution in the United States

Anybody undertaking even the most cursory examination of the death penalty as it has operated in the United States cannot fail to notice one glaringly obvious fact, namely that black people and members of other ethnic minorities are far more likely to be hanged, gassed, electrocuted, shot or given lethal injections than white people. A few examples will make this a little clearer.

The largest mass execution in American history, and incidentally the greatest number of people ever to be hanged simultaneously anywhere in the world, took place in the Minnesota city of Mankato in 1862. On that occasion, no fewer than thirty-eight members of the Dakota tribe were hanged from a single enormous scaffold. They had been found guilty of waging war against settlers and the US Army. In the twentieth century it was predominantly black people who appeared to be over-represented in the statistics for capital punishment in America. The last person to be publicly executed, in Kentucky in 1936, was a young black man called Rainey Bethea. He had been sentenced to death for rape. In the United Kingdom there were no executions for any offence other than murder or treason from the middle of the nineteenth century onwards. The situation was very different in America. Just five years after Rainey Bethea was publicly hanged, a 22-year-old man died in Alabama's electric chair for burglary. Like Bethea, Frank Bass was an African American and on 8 August 1941, he became the last person to be executed for this offence in the United States. In the decade before Bass' execution, ten other men had been executed for burglary. Every one of them was black. It was a similar story with other types of capital crime, with black men being grossly over-represented in all groups.

Between 1930 and 1964, a total of twenty-five men were executed in the United States for armed robbery. Of these, nineteen were black and just six white. The statistics for rape are even starker. Between 1930 and 1964, there were 455 executions for rape; 405 of these men were black. Notable individual executions are also alarmingly likely to feature African Americans. In 1944, the youngest person executed in twentieth-century America died in South Carolina's electric chair. It is almost beyond belief, but George Junius Stinney was just 14 years of age when he died. He was so small that a thick book had to be used as a booster seat so that the straps of the electric chair could be fastened around him. The black teenager had been convicted of murder, a verdict which has since been quashed. George Stinney was not the only teenager to face the electric chair in the 1940s. Another African American youth was sentenced to death at the age of 16 for a crime committed when he was just 15 years of age. He achieved fame as the only person in history to survive electrocution in the electric chair.

In late 1944 a pharmacist in Louisiana was shot and killed in what was assumed to be a robbery. Nine months later, a 16-year-old boy called Willie Francis was arrested for an unrelated matter and found to have the pharmacist's wallet in his possession. He made two written confessions to the murder, was tried, found guilty and sentenced to die in the electric chair. At that time the State of Louisiana had a mobile electric chair which was moved from prison to prison and then set up and wired to the electricity supply as the need arose. The nickname of this apparatus was 'Gruesome Gertie'. On 3 May 1946 Willie Francis, who had turned 17 just a few months earlier, was scheduled to die in 'Gruesome Gertie'.

We saw in a previous chapter how the last public execution in the United States was marred by the executioner being drunk. A similar thing happened when the first attempt was made to electrocute Willie Francis. The night before the execution, the electric chair was set up by two men. The official executioner was Captain Ephie Foster and he was helped by a prison inmate named Vincent Venezia. Unfortunately, both men were drinking heavily as they prepared for the execution and as a result, the wiring was incorrectly connected.

With his head shaved, in order that better contact could be made with the electrode, Willie Francis was strapped into the electric chair on the day of his execution and the switch thrown. The result was not his death, but rather a great deal of suffering. A strong current surged through the young man's body, but it was nowhere nearly strong enough to kill him. He thrashed about in agony, shouting for the facemask used during such executions to be removed. Eventually, when it became obvious that he was not going to die, the current was switched off and he was removed from the chair. Enormously irritated and embarrassed, the bungling executioner shouted, 'I missed you this time, but I'll get you next week if I have to use a rock!' Despite a spirited appeal to the courts, Willie Francis, by that time 18, was successfully executed in the same electric chair a year later.

We have looked a little at some executions involving black people in this way to provide a little context for the administration of justice in the US Army which led to a grossly disproportionate number of black and Hispanic men being executed in Britain, as opposed to the number of white men who suffered similarly. There was unease about this situation among members of the British Parliament and others, but their anxieties were quieted, sometimes by the provision of misleading or false information.

To understand why so many black and Hispanic prisoners found guilty of murder, rape, burglary and armed robbery were being executed in the United States in the period at which we are looking, we must consider an aspect of the American judicial system which differed greatly from that of the United Kingdom. Under British law, some criminal offences were known as 'capital crimes'. In this context, the word 'capital' relates to the Latin word for head and indicates that the life of a person convicted of such an offence was forfeit. There was no leeway about this, neither the judge nor jury having any say in the sentence passed. A man or woman who had been convicted of murder, espionage in wartime or high treason would be sentenced to death and there was an end to the matter. There was the possibility of a reprieve by the Home Secretary and the substitution of a sentence of imprisonment for life, but this was not a particularly common occurrence.

In America, in both civilian courts and courts martial during the Second World War, the situation was quite different. Death was available as a penalty, but not mandatory. In other words, if the judges at a court martial felt that the defendant was a particularly vicious piece of work, then they might have been more inclined to impose the death penalty rather than imprisonment. In ordinary courts in the United States, even to this day, there is a process whereby after convicting a prisoner of murder, the jury may have a second consultation to decide upon the penalty. This, it needs hardly be said, gives ample opportunity for any latent prejudice to operate.

There are two very important differences between executions as they have always operated in the United States and the way in which they were conducted in Britain up to the last hanging, which took place in 1964. These are both relevant to the subject of this book, because they explain why hangings in America failed to develop and evolve further than the fixed drop and traditional 'cowboy coil' type of noose. Put simply, rather than persevere and make their hangings more sophisticated, Americans chose by and large to abandon the practice and invent what they saw as more up-to-date and modern ways to dispose of murderers and rapists.

In Britain, because it is so much smaller than the United States, it was practical to have only one or two official executioners who went to any part of the country where they were needed to carry out their duties. Whenever a man or woman needed to be hanged anywhere in the British Isles, it was only necessary for the hangman, wherever he lived, to take a short journey by railway and he could be at the prison in a matter of hours. Such an arrangement would hardly have been practical in America in the nineteenth and early twentieth centuries. For an executioner in New York to travel across the continent to San

Francisco to hang somebody would have seemed a needless expense and an awful waste of time. There were the also the sensitivities of the individual states to consider. It is to be doubted if a prison in Georgia would have welcomed effusively a New Yorker arriving to hang one of their citizens! For these reasons, those responsible for executions by hanging tended to be local men, often with little grasp of the technicalities involved in breaking somebody's neck efficiently.

Something which may not be appreciated fully today is that ensuring a hanging went smoothly and killed the victim neatly and immediately needed considerable planning. Those wishing to become executioners in Britain had to attend a residential course at one of the London prisons which had gallows installed in them. There, they were expected to study not just the practical part of the process, measuring the drop and adjusting the rope around the neck, but also to master the necessary theoretical aspects, such as the mathematical calculations needed to make sure that the correct drop was given. This ensured that when a British hangman carried out an execution, the condemned prisoner neither choked to death nor was his or her head ripped off. At the end of this gruelling five-day course, the candidate would have to sit a written examination, at which nothing less than a 100 per cent mark was required. Below is the paper taken in 1940 by a man called Stephen Wade, who was a hangman in Britain for a decade or so after the end of the Second World War. It includes the answers which he gave

Q. What is the reason for leaving the sand-bag suspended on the rope during the night preceding the morning of the execution?
A. To stretch the rope to ensure that a perfect measure of the drop should be obtained.

Q. What measurement is allowed for a culprit's neck?
A. Thirteen inches.

Q. Why is the copper wire used when 'setting' up the rope to the drop?
A. As a definite marking, which would not otherwise be obtained, when the sand-bag is left from the trap, owing to the shrinkage of the rope ensuring the definite marking of the culprit's height.

Q. Give the length of drop you would state for a man of 158lbs
A. 6ft 3ins. The weight of the culprit is divided into 1,000. Weight of culprit 158lbs into 1,000 = 158/1,000 5ft 8/9 = 5ft 6ins + 9 ins as required by the new 1913 regulations.

In addition to the strict training and examinations which anybody wishing to be an executioner in Britain was obliged to undergo, they then had to serve what amounted to an apprenticeship. That is to say that they would need to spend a few years as assistant executioners. This meant attending executions, although at first their role was restricted to strapping the prisoner's hands behind his or her back before the hangman took over. This meant that any prospective executioner would know the business inside out and have been present at many hangings before being given the opportunity to carry out an execution himself.

By all of this it will be seen that the British system was very different from that operating in the United States, where executioners often took on the job for a few extra dollars and because nobody else could be found who was willing to undertake the task. We saw earlier that even at public executions, the hangman might be inebriated and this tells us something about the quality of executioners available. One wonders how many of such men would be capable of dividing 158lbs by 1,000, translating the answer into feet and inches and then adjusting the drop accordingly!

Of course, the British hangmen were also working at an advantage because the design of the gallows which they used was standardized, to make it easier to adjust the length of the drop. The rope was attached to a length of stout chain and this could be moved up and down to vary the distance that the victim would fall. American gallows differed enormously from one prison to another. Many were constructed so that only a fixed drop was possible. In the late nineteenth century, thought was given to designing a new and more efficient type of gallows, but this did not work out well, as we shall see. Let us turn now to another important advantage of British executions, the presence or absence of witnesses.

On 26 May 1868, an Irish terrorist called Michael Barrett was publicly hanged in London. This was the last such execution in the United Kingdom. From then on all hangings would take place privately within prisons. At first a small number of newspaper reporters were allowed to witness the executions, but this did not last long and by the end of the nineteenth century only those officially concerned with the execution in some capacity were allowed to be present. There was a legal prohibition on revealing any details of what occurred during a hanging and the Home Office threatened to prosecute former executioners if they later spoke of their experiences. This was not because anything alarming or discreditable was taking place, but simply because it was felt better for all concerned if the whole thing remained private.

In America, public executions continued until the eve of the Second World War and even executions which were nominally held in private often had large crowds watching them. When Eva Dugan was accidentally decapitated in 1930, almost 100 people saw it happen. Such public and semi-public hangings played a role in preventing executioners in the United States from adopting new and improved techniques and in particular using a carefully-calculated long drop such as would infallibly break the neck of the prisoner every time. Instead, there was a move to abandon traditional hangings entirely and find new ways to inflict the death penalty. This meant that those hangings which continued into the middle of the twentieth century followed the same antiquated procedure which had been used to despatch the so-called 'Lincoln Conspirators'.

The problem was that when many people saw a botched hanging in which the victim was slowly strangled or, worse still, decapitated, there was a natural revulsion and lurid accounts written by journalists who had been invited to be present at the event appeared in the newspapers. The reaction to such gruesome stories was not a determination to change radically the way that hangings were carried out and train executioners how to work out the best drop. Instead, the search began for simpler methods of execution which would require no complicated sums or special training and would make the deaths of the condemned prisoners less horrible to watch. The first such invention was a new type of gallows which did away with the drop entirely and was promised to revolutionize hanging. The new invention would, it was claimed, snap the neck every time without any fuss and hard work on the part of the hangman. Indeed, one ingenious version of this gadget even did away with the need for an executioner entirely and was supposed to break a man or woman's neck without anybody having to pull a lever and initiate the process.

The first innovation in the construction of gallows since the invention of the long drop came in America in the early 1880s, with the development of what became known colloquially as the 'jerk-'em-up' system of hanging. It was thought by some that if a neck could be broken by dropping somebody with a rope around the neck for some distance, then precisely the same effect could be achieved if instead of letting the person fall, the rope itself was suddenly given a great jerk upwards. It was, superficially at least, a plausible notion but in practice hardly ever worked. Just as with the fixed drop of a traditional gallows, which of the condemned men and women strangled slowly and painfully and which died swiftly was largely a matter of chance.

The 'jerk-'em-up' method relied upon the use of a pulley and a very heavy weight, typically about 350lbs or 400lbs. This was dropped from a height, with the rope attached to it. The rope ran over a pulley in a beam above the condemned person and as it fell, the other end of the rope, which was of course secured around the neck of the victim, was jerked up very sharply. To see how this extraordinary arrangement worked in practice, we cannot do better than look at a specific example, one which was to have far-reaching effects upon the way in which capital punishment in the United States was carried out in the twentieth century.

New York was keen to avoid the awful spectacle of people choking to death at the end of a rope and so in the 1880s installed a 'jerk-'em-up' gallows, sometimes also known as an 'upright jerker'. Those suffering death by means of this new device were jocularly said in prisons to have been 'jerked to Jesus'. The results of the gallows were disappointing. Some victims had their necks broken by it; many did not. There was increasing disquiet about the 'upright jerker', for it did not seem to be much of an improvement on old gallows. On 28 February 1887 a hanging occurred which was to precipitate another change is the mode of execution used in New York. This was the date when a woman called Roxana Druse died.

Roxana Druse had murdered her husband and spent a couple of years fighting through the courts to save her own life. By the autumn of 1887, all legal avenues had been exhausted and her only hope was a commutation of sentence. None came and so she was taken to the gallows in front of a crowd of witnesses, including a number of newspaper reporters. Not only was her neck not cleanly snapped when she was pulled suddenly and violently into the air, but Roxana Druse spent at least 15 minutes spinning and writhing as she struggled for breath, making ghastly moaning sounds. To use an expression current at the time, 'she died hard'. Because so many people were present, it was impossible to hush up what had happened and there was public outrage at the thought of a woman being slowly tortured to death in this way. A more humane means of putting people to death was sought and this led to the construction of the world's first electric chair. There were to be only two more executions with the 'upright jerker' before William Kemmler became the first person in the world to suffer death by judicial electrocution in 1890.

New York provides us with a classic illustration of the process which took place across much of the United States in the 50 years between 1880 and 1930, as one state after another rejected the fixed–drop gallows in favour of other methods of capital punishment. It seemed so much easier to look for a more modern and up-to-date way of executing criminals, rather than simply working on and perfecting the existing method, which would have entailed studying how the long drop worked and training men in its use.

Of course, if there had not been so many witnesses to the bungling efforts of American executioners to break their clients' necks, then none of this would have mattered. The clamour from the public, who could not be expected fully to understand the finer points of hanging, was that hanging was brutal and barbaric and that some other means would have to be found for disposing of murderers and rapists. This is why, despite its ineffective and cruel use in America, no changes were ever made in the way that hanging was carried out. It was easier just to give up the practice entirely and switch to something else.

The desire for novelty and modernity in modes of execution had a deleterious effect on hanging in the United States. The electric chair sounded very up-to-date and modern, so it became for a while the most fashionable way of disposing of criminals who had been sentenced to death. The smell of burning human flesh put some people off this method, however, and so in 1924 the gas chamber began to be used. This was felt to be a much more hygienic and clinical way of killing people, and like the electric chair soon replaced the gallows in a number of states. A consequence of this was that as the gallows was sidelined as a method of inflicting capital punishment, so it became neglected and nobody saw any reason to try and improve it. It was on the way out anyway; why tinker around with it? This meant that hanging was not developed and modified in the way that was constantly happening in Britain. It remained stuck in the nineteenth century, with the 'cowboy coil' and fixed drop. For that reason alone, it could not hope to compete in efficiency or humanity with the way that the British conducted their own hangings.

This lengthy excursion into the history of capital punishment in the United States during the twentieth century has been necessary to explain first why America never took the same path as Britain did, which is to say perfecting hanging as a means of execution. It has also shown us why the British authorities, however relaxed and easy-going they might be about allowing the US Army to sidestep the law of Britain entirely and take responsibility for trying their own capital cases, were utterly implacable about the matter of the execution itself. It is time now to see how this peculiar arrangement worked in practice. In the next chapter we shall look in great detail at the circumstances surrounding the first of the American executions to be carried out at Shepton Mallet.

Chapter 6

The First Execution at Shepton Mallet

I n 1921 just over 10,000 people lived in the town of Dothan, in the southern American state of Alabama. Roughly a third of those living in the town were black and their lives were strictly bound by the so-called 'Jim Crow' laws which enforced segregation along racial lines. Buses, cinemas, restaurants and all public facilities had sections for whites and others for those who were black or of mixed race. Lynchings were still a feature of life in the Deep South at that time. Even so, some black people had better lives than others and were born with greater opportunities for advancement. Being the child of professional people gave one then, as now, a distinct advantage.

The Reverend Howard C. Cobb was a black clergyman, who lived in Dothan with his wife Addie Mae and son Richard. Churches too were segregated at that time and the Reverend Cobb was minister at an exclusively black church. His was a respectable career though and he was an educated man. When, on 14 November 1921, his wife gave birth to a second son, Howard Cobb probably felt that his life was as good as it could be for a black man at that time and in that particular part of the United States. The boy was named David.

Nobody knows why some children turn out bad. Certainly, young David Cobb had an excellent start in life, at least compared to his contemporaries, but somehow he was always getting into mischief and unable to settle down and work at school. A frequent truant, he finally gave up school at the age of 14 and picked up work in a newspaper distribution company. From an early age, he acquired a taste for drinking and as a teenager his older brother often had to bring him home after he had drunk himself into a state of insensibility. Anybody less in a position to be able to marry and support a wife it would be hard to imagine, but nevertheless in 1938, at the age of 16, this is just what David Cobb did. It was what was known in those days as a 'shotgun wedding', the girl being already pregnant and David facing a choice between marrying his young girlfriend or facing the vengeance of her father. Having no place of his own and lacking the money to rent anywhere, he installed his new bride, Cornelia Dozier, in his parents' home, where she soon gave birth. His first child was a boy, whom he named Howard, after his father. A daughter called Christine soon followed. The strain of living with her in-laws eventually became too much for Cornelia and she returned to her parents' home with her children.

This then was David Cobb's life at the end of 1941. He had just turned 20 years of age, still living with his parents and with a failed marriage behind him and two children who needed to be supported financially in some way. The Japanese attack on Pearl Harbor, which took place just three weeks after David Cobb's 20th birthday, made it very likely that he would soon be called up for army service. Like all young men, he had already been registered for selective service and rather than simply wait until he was actually conscripted, Cobb enlisted in the army voluntarily on 8 January 1942. At the time, it must have seemed like the perfect way of evading his responsibilities and removing himself as far as possible from his previous life. After basic training at Fort Dix in New Jersey, he was assigned to the 827th Engineer Battalion. At a stroke, the shiftless and irresponsible young man had been transformed into one of those who would avenge the humiliation of Pearl Harbor and fight for his country.

There is of course a saying in the Bible which touches upon the improbability of a leopard changing its spots, which in the case of David Cobb proved only too true. He had led a wild and undisciplined life up to then; why would anybody expect him to change now, simply because he had donned a uniform?

During 1942, David Cobb managed to avoid a court martial, there being a tendency on the part of senior officers to be a little easy on the young men who had volunteered to go to war in Europe and the

Pacific. He was confined to barracks for various minor infractions, but nothing serious was recorded against him. It was not until his unit was sent to England on 16 December 1942 that disaster struck. By this time, Cobb had had more than enough of army life and soon after arriving at Desborough Camp in Northamptonshire he was disciplined for his sloppy appearance on parade and confined to barracks. Conduct which might be tolerated at a training camp is likely to be viewed with greater severity in a country which is actually at war, as was the case in England at that time.

Being confined to barracks meant little to David Cobb, other than to increase the sense of grievance which he felt against the US Army. On the night of 26 December, just 11 days after arriving in England, Cobb was allocated to night duty in the guardhouse. His shift was supposed to last from 10:00 pm until 6:00 am the following day. However, at 10:30 on the morning of 27 December, he had not been relieved. This kind of thing is an unfortunate feature of wartime and most soldiers simply accept it as an annoyance. This was not the case with David Cobb and when an officer turned up at the guardhouse, he made his feelings clear. Lieutenant Robert J. Cobner was not much older than Cobb at 25 years of age. He was the Battalion Officer of the Day and had come to the guardhouse with two other men, one a sergeant, intending to move some beds around.

Rather than carrying his rifle in the regulation way, on his shoulder, the discontented Cobb had it casually draped across his shoulders and he spoke to the young officer in a way which suggested that he had little respect for him. Specifically, he complained that he had been on duty for too long and wasn't going to carry on any longer. Lieutenant Cobner told him to hold his rifle properly and stand to attention, because he was addressing an officer. He then told Cobb that if he did not improve his manner, then he was liable to find himself on a charge. This had no effect upon the angry soldier, who remarked that he was already confined to barracks, adding, as was testified to at the subsequent court martial, 'I ain't staying at this post no longer.' Hearing this defiance,

Lieutenant Cobner ordered his sergeant to arrest Cobb, who at this point brought his rifle down from his shoulders and aimed it at the sergeant, who prudently backed away. Cobb said that he would not relinquish his weapon to anybody until he was properly relieved. This later turned into a key point of Cobb's defence against the charge of murder which he faced.

There was little that Cobner could do now, except attempt to disarm David Cobb himself and take him into custody. As he moved towards the angry young man, there was a single shot, whereupon Lieutenant Cobner fell dead with a bullet through his heart. After shooting the young officer, Cobb pointed his rifle at the sergeant and other soldiers present and told them to place Cobner's body in the nearby jeep. He then asked if there was anybody present who did not like what he had done. The other men prudently remained silent.

On 6 January 1943, just 10 days after the incident, David Cobb faced a court martial in Cambridge. He pleaded not guilty to murder and his defence was an ingenious one. He said that he had been on guard duty that day and that he understood that the correct procedure for relieving a person from that duty was for an NCO to bring a replacement and inform the man on duty that he might leave his post. According to Cobb's testimony, he had asked the sergeant who was with Lieutenant Cobner when he might have a relief, as he had been on duty for a long while and wished to eat. Cobner had then apparently, answered the question for the sergeant, saying that he didn't care how long Cobb had been on duty. He then ordered the sergeant to take Cobb's rifle. Whereupon, according to his statement, Cobb had said to the sergeant as he approached him, 'You can't give me an order where you can take that gun on this post, remember I am on guard'. In short, Cobb claimed to be strictly following the regulations relating to guards on duty. He agreed that Lieutenant Cobner had taken a few paces towards him, saying, 'Soldier, give me that gun!'

The question inevitably arose as to why he had shot the officer who asked for his gun. Cobb's position was that he had not been aware that

Lieutenant Cobner had been Officer of the Day. Had he known this, then he would have handed over his weapon to him. It was an unusual defence, but it all fell apart once Cobb was on the witness stand. He said that it was not his intention to kill anybody and he had hoped to hit Lieutenant Cobner in the hip, rather than the heart. The moment which really destroyed his case though was when he was asked about the substance of the General Orders, which he had said laid down the correct procedure for relieving a guard on duty. Not only was he unable to quote the relevant sections, he appeared to know nothing at all about them.

David Cobb was found guilty and was sentenced to death for murdering an officer who had been performing his duty. After an appeal and review of his sentence, it was confirmed that David Cobb was to be hanged at Shepton Mallet Prison on 12 March 1943. The execution of 21-year-old Private Cobb was to be the first test of the peculiar arrangement which had been put together, whereby American soldiers would be tried by American courts, but executed by an Englishman.

Because, as we saw in an earlier chapter, hanging in Britain had been developed until it was almost an art, there was a tendency for the role of hangman to run in families, passed down from father to son. This way, the tricks of the trade could be transmitted from one generation to the next. Members of these dynasties were often chosen by the prison authorities in preference to those who might be termed 'outsiders'. In France, much the same thing happened with the famous Sanson family. Two such families in Britain were the Billingtons and the Pierrepoints. James Billington was a hangman from 1884 until his death in 1901. His three sons, Thomas, William and John, all served as hangmen as well. The Billingtons are not as well-known as the Pierrepoints – Henry, Thomas and Albert. Between them, these three men carried out hundreds of executions in the United Kingdom over the course of over half a century.

Henry Pierrepoint became a hangman in 1901, assisting James Billington at one of the last executions he performed before his death that year. After sharing the role of executioner with Billington's three sons, Henry Pierrepoint persuaded his brother Thomas to join him. For the next 40 years, Thomas Pierrepoint was the principal executioner operating in Britain. In 1931, Henry's son Albert joined his uncle Thomas as an assistant hangman, his father having retired by then. It was Thomas Pierrepoint who was called upon by the Americans to carry out the first hanging of a US serviceman at Shepton Mallet. He was assisted by his nephew Albert. A fuller and more detailed account of the lives of these two executioners is to be found in Appendix 3.

Thomas Pierrepoint had been to Shepton Mallet before. It was he who carried out the last civilian execution at the prison, which had taken place 17 years earlier. On that occasion, John Lincoln had been hanged for murdering a man in the course of a bungled robbery (see Chapter 3).

Thomas Pierrepoint was 72 years old when he undertook that first military execution at Shepton Mallet and had been carrying out executions for almost 40 years. He may be seen in Illustration 11. There was no indication that his advancing age was having any deleterious effect upon his ability to hang people, although he was certainly a little brusquer and less patient than had once been the case. More than one prison governor had actually complained about him in recent years, although the Home Office, which was responsible for hiring executioners, gave these men short shrift. Less than three months before he hanged David Cobb, the governor of London's Wandsworth Prison had written to the Prison Commission, expressing his concerns. In a letter dated 11 November 1942, he stated that;

> At the execution of a recent prisoner on 6.11.42 I was not favourably impressed by the attitude of T. W. Pierrepoint the executioner.
>
> The execution was carried out with expedition and satisfactorily performed. I have the greatest admiration for the way in which the Minister prepared the prisoner for his end, and the comfort the latter receives from the former

enables him, in average cases, to meet his end with admirable decorum.But if the end of the Minister's influence over the prisoner is brought to a close too abruptly, a more unhappy scene is witnessed than, in my opinion is necessary.

I formed the opinion that Mr. Pierrepoint at his advanced age, I believe his age is 72 years – has passed his peak of efficiency and is becoming less tactful and more abrupt in his methods. It impressed me as though he had turned what I would call an unpleasant episode of drastic efficiency, into a more unpleasant one.

B.E.N. Grew
Governor.

The reply from the Prison Commission was exceedingly curt, making reference to the 'difficulty of wartime replacements'. In short, they told the governor of Wandsworth Prison that there was a war on and he would just have to make do with whatever executioners were available. We may assume that the US Army knew nothing of all this and were simply minded to accept whoever they were sent to carry out their executions for them.

Thomas Pierrepoint and his nephew arrived at Shepton Mallet Prison on the afternoon of Thursday, 11 March. They were to find that American executions differed in two important respects from those which they were accustomed to carry out. They were certainly able to calculate the correct drop and use the British type of noose, with a free-running eyelet at the end. This would ensure that the condemned man would have his neck neatly snapped, rather than having the possibility of choking to death at the end of the rope. However, they learned two disturbing things. The first was that the execution had to be conducted at the first hour of the designated day, rather than at eight or nine in the morning, as was usual for British executions. This was not a great problem, as they usually prepared the gallows for the execution on the afternoon and evening before a hanging. The second difference was a little more difficult for them to adapt to.

The whole practical aim of British executions was to ensure that the condemned prisoner was hanged as soon as humanly possible after the executioners entered his cell. In some prisons the execution chamber was adjacent to the condemned cell, but in others it was a short walk away. From entering the cell until the man or woman was hanging at the end of the rope typically took no more than 15 or 20 seconds. Albert Pierrepoint managed on occasion to whittle this time down to seven seconds, surely a world record. Albert Pierrepoint, who went on to become the world's most industrious and prolific hangman, may be seen in Illustration 12. One person who acted as an assistant executioner alongside Albert Pierrepoint said that he would light a cigar before going to hang a prisoner. By the time it was all over and he returned to the room where he had been staying, the cigar would still be smouldering and Pierrepoint only needed to draw upon it in order to make the end glow. It was an impressive, if rather gruesome, party piece. There was though a very good reason for the extraordinary celerity with which both Tom and Albert Pierrepoint conducted executions.

The strain of knowing that one is about to die is tremendous and even the strongest and most self-controlled of us might be prone to fainting or even a bout of hysteria as the fatal moment draws near. The procedure was to give the victim as little chance as possible to think about what was happening. The executioner and his assistant entered the cell, moved swiftly to strap the hands behind the back and then hurried the man or woman to the nearby scaffold. In most British prisons, the execution chamber was actually next door to the condemned cell. This meant that while the hangman entered the cell, a prison warder was moving aside a bookcase which concealed the door to the room where the noose was ready and waiting. The speed of the operation, to which the governor of Wandsworth Prison objected, was really a kindness. The whole business was over and done with before the condemned prisoner had any time properly to consider what was happening. The American way was very different.

The Pierrepoints were horrified to learn that once they had pinioned the man they were to hang and led him to the scaffold, they would be obliged to wait before putting the hood over his head, the rope round his neck and operating the trapdoor. This was so that the sentence of death could be read once more to the man standing and waiting to be executed and the whole process by which his appeals for clemency had been denied explained to him in detail. He would then be given the opportunity to make a final statement, if he wished to do so. The entire, ghastly process lasted for about five minutes. After his retirement, Albert Pierrepoint wrote of this:

> The part of the routine which I found it hardest to acclimatise myself to was the, to me, sickening interval between my introduction to the prisoner and his death. Under British custom I was working to the sort of timing where the drop fell between eight and twenty seconds after I had entered the condemned's cell. Under the American system, after I had pinioned the prisoner, he had to stand on the drop for perhaps six minutes while his charge sheet was read out, sentence spelt out, and he was asked if he had anything to say, and after that I was instructed to get on with the job.

In accordance with American practice, David Cobb's execution took place at 1:00 am on 12 March. The young man, who it will be recalled was just 21 years of age, marched calmly to the scaffold and stood there stoically while the various formalities were concluded. While the official statements were being made, the chaplain continued to pray out loud in the background. At last, Thomas Pierrepoint was given the signal and pulled the lever which released the trapdoor.

One point which might puzzle anybody who has ever actually visited the execution chamber in which sixteen men were hanged is how it was possible to squeeze so many people into such a small space without anybody tumbling by accident through the trapdoor. Look again at Illustration 9, which shows the room as it is now. It is about the size of an average bedroom and yet according some accounts, up to twenty people would have been crammed in here when an execution was to take place. And even when everything was ready, there was no question of just pulling the lever and finishing the job. Everybody stood around in the cramped room for five or ten minutes until the rigmarole of reading the charges out had been undertaken. How it might have been during one of the double executions performed here, when the reading of the charges and sentences would have taken twice as long, does not bear thinking about.

One final point about the ritual involved in the military executions carried out by the US Army has yet to be mentioned. This was an ignominious death and it was felt to be salutary for all concerned to be reminded of the fact. Soldiers who had been sentenced to death were, before their execution, dishonourably discharged from the army. This meant that when they were hanged or shot, they wore uniforms with all badges and insignia torn off or otherwise removed. Why not simply let them die in their own clothes? There would be a risk then that the condemned prisoner might arrived for his date with the hangman or firing squad looking dapper and smart, which would never do. The whole point was that he should appear to be degraded and obviously somebody who had been thrown out of the army.

This then was the first of the eighteen executions which would be carried out at Shepton Mallet. In civilian executions in Britain at that time, the bodies of those hanged were buried in unmarked graves within the prison grounds, but the Americans were not concerned with the disposal of the corpse and so Cobb was buried in Brookwood Cemetery in Surrey. After the war, in March 1949, his widow arranged for the body to be exhumed and reburied in the United States. He now lies in next to his sister Ruby in Dothlan's North Highland Street cemetery.

An execution at a fictionalized version of Shepton Mallet Prison during the war was portrayed in the 1967 film *The Dirty Dozen*, which starred Donald Sutherland, Charles Bronson and Lee Marvin. The prison is renamed Marston-Tyne in the film and many details of the hanging shown are wildly inaccurate. The condemned man walks along a traditional American death row, for example, and the hood which is placed on his head is black, rather than the white one actually used in such executions in this country. Weirdly, there is no executioner, the whole procedure is conducted by military personnel, with an American Military Policeman even pulling the lever to release the trapdoor. Intriguingly though, a Military Policeman *did* operate the gallows at some American executions in Europe. Joseph Malta, a 28-year-old Military Policeman, offered to assist official hangman John Woods in executing the major Nazi war criminals at Nuremberg in October 1946.

This first hanging was to be followed by fifteen more. At every one of these executions, Thomas Pierrepoint was the executioner, almost invariably assisted by his nephew Albert. We will look in a later chapter at the murders which led to most of these executions, but in the next chapter we will consider those cases where men were hanged for rape, sometimes carried out at the same time as murder. Although in Britain it had been almost a century since anybody had been executed for anything other than murder, treason or espionage, under American military law, the offence of rape was a capital crime, although it had not carried the death penalty in Britain since 1841.

Chapter 7

Three Rapists

On a bitterly cold Tuesday morning towards the end of January 1835, 26-year-old Mark Devlin was publicly hanged in the Scottish city of Dundee. According to spectators at the execution, he was a good-looking young man. Mark Devlin had been condemned to death for the rape of 13-year-old Ann MacLachlan and he was one of the last men to be hanged for this offence in Britain. Six years after his execution, the death penalty for rape would be abolished.

In the early years of the nineteenth century, over 200 crimes were punishable by death in Britain. These were the days of the so-called 'Bloody Code', when hanging was believed to be a sure deterrent to any kind of crime. Offences carrying the death penalty ranged from murder and rape to burglary and arson. Even such trifling matters as consorting with gypsies or defacing London's Westminster Bridge could, at least in theory, lead to the scaffold. It is not savage punishments though which deter criminals, but rather the likelihood of being caught. With the establishment of properly organized police forces, it was found that crime rates fell, as those minded to break the law realized that the odds of getting away with robberies or rapes were shortening. As this happened, the number of crimes attracting the death penalty began to drop. By the middle of the century, there remained only a handful of capital crimes. In practice, the only executions which took place by the 1860s were for murder. Because it has been so long since anybody has been executed in Britain for anything except murder or, in very rare cases, treason, it is sometimes assumed that the same holds true for most other Western countries. It is not really so, at least as far as the United States is concerned. As late as 1964, rapists were being executed in America and the last execution for burglary took place in 1942.

The arrangement whereby a British executioner hanged men in England for crimes committed which were contrary to the military code of the United States gave rise to a bizarre situation in which a British executioner was hanging people for something which had not been a capital offence in Britain for over a century. There was some disquiet about this state of affairs, but little that could be done about it. Once it had been agreed that American soldiers in Britain would not be bound by the laws of this country, then it was obvious that they would have to be subject to some other legal system. United States military personnel in the United Kingdom were subject to The Articles of War from 1920. According to these, 'Any person subject to military law who commits murder or rape shall suffer death or imprisonment for life'. It was, at least on the face of it, as simple as that. Of course, the devil, as always, was in the detail. In this case the detail was who would be charged with rape in the first place and then, if convicted, who would be chosen to hang and who to serve time in prison.

We have seen in Chapter 5 that the American penal system appeared to be heavily weighted against non-white people. They were more likely to be arrested than whites, more likely to be charged and, if convicted of sexual offences, far more likely to suffer the severest punishment. This regrettable tendency was clearly visible in the treatment of those convicted of rape by American courts martial held in the United Kingdom during the Second World War. In total, there were 126 convictions for this offence between 1942 and 1945. Just six men were sentenced to death and executed, however. Five were black and one Hispanic. No white man faced the supreme penalty available to those applying the law. Again, this simply mirrored the situation at home in the United States, where the great majority of those executed for rape in the years between 1930 and 1964, 405 out of 455, were African Americans.

The execution of American soldiers for rape, and the possibility that these hangings had been motivated by racial prejudice, was raised in the House of Commons on 6 July 1944, as some Members of Parliament were growing uneasy about the situation. Rhys Davies, the MP for Westhoughton, said that;

> Early this year I saw a very brief notice in our Press that a negro soldier belonging to the United States Army had been sentenced to death by an American court-martial in this country, for an offence against a woman living in Burton-on-Trent. The woman, so far as I know, is still alive. It occurred to me a rather strange state of affairs that any person should be so sentenced on British soil for an offence that is not punishable with the extreme penalty under our own law.

The fact that he specifically mentioned that the soldier concerned had been black was enough to indicate which way Rhys Davies' mind was working. He went on to say;

> Sentence of death, or capital punishment, does not apply in every one of the States of the United States, and it is quite possible, therefore, to have an American court-martial in this country sentencing to death a negro for an offence for which he would not be so sentenced in his own State in his own land. Another point to be borne in mind in this connection is that America is the only Power in this country that adopts this method. We have the Czech, Belgian, Norwegian and other Governments here, and I understand that not one of those Governments applies any of its laws in such a way as to violate our own legal code. I do not want to dwell unduly upon this subject, but I wish there were a Minister present to answer me.

Home Secretary Herbert Morrison had already spoken to the Judge Advocate General's office in London about the possibility that black soldiers were the subject of discrimination when it came to sentencing and although he was not aware of it, they caused him to mislead the House of Commons by dismissing the concerns of MPs. Indeed, he reproved them for sowing dissent and causing trouble. A senior American official had told the Home Secretary that there was no prejudice and that the Americans would be happy if the Home Secretary would tell anybody who asked that three white soldiers had been sentenced to death for rape in America a year before. This was misleading, as at the time that the conversation took place, only black soldiers in Britain had been condemned to death for rape.

Perhaps it is time to examine one or two specific cases of rape for which the death penalty was imposed at Shepton Mallet. We begin with the first person executed for rape in Britain since the 1830s. Lee Davis, a 22-year-old black soldier, stationed in Wiltshire, was found guilty of murder as well as rape, which meant that under the laws of Britain he would also have been liable to hang for his crimes. Davis may be seen in Illustration 13.

On the evening of Tuesday, 28 September 1943, two young women bumped into each other outside the cinema in the Wiltshire town of Marlborough. They found that they had both just finished watching the same film. Cynthia June Lay and Muriel Fawden knew each other; both lived and worked at the nearby Savernake Hospital. It was a pleasant evening and still light, so they decided to walk back to the hospital together. Cynthia, more generally known as June, Lay was 18 and Muriel 22. It was only eight o'clock and walking along the country road to the hospital seemed safe enough. As they neared the hospital, an American soldier armed with a rifle appeared behind them. They had no idea where he had come from. He asked the two girls where they were going. They replied that they were going to the nearby hospital and both began walking a little more briskly, in the hope of getting away from the man. Then they heard a shouted command to stand still or be shot. Both froze in terror.

The man with the rifle told the two of them to enter a field next to the road, but they pointed out that it would mean climbing through a tangle of barbed wire. There was something in this, so they were instructed to walk back along the road, in the direction from which they had come. It was obvious by now that the man was intended to harm them in some way and so the younger of the two women, June Lay, shouted to her friend that they should make a run for it. She began haring down the road as fast as she was able. At this point, the soldier raised his rifle and opened fire. Two bullets struck June Lay in the back, killing her instantly. The man then fired a couple of shots over Muriel Fawden's head, in an attempt to frighten her into submission. It worked and he was able to drag the unresisting young woman into a field and rape her twice.

Darkness had now fallen and men with torches were searching the nearby fields and woods, June Lay's body having been discovered by a passing driver. Fully expecting that she too would be murdered, the woman who had been raped initiated a dialogue with her captor, explaining that she was a Christian and able to forgive him for what he had done. This touched a chord in the man who had carried out the brutal attack, because he then offered to see her safely home, on the grounds that it might not be safe for her to walk alone through the dark countryside. He escorted her to the grounds of the hospital where she worked and then bade her goodnight in the most natural way in the world.

It was not difficult to track down the black soldier whom Muriel Fawden described. Private Lee Davis, stationed on a nearby American base, had not been in his bunk when an officer conducted a routine check at 11:30 pm that day. He had no permission to leave the base and nobody knew where he had gone. By the time he returned, the officer in charge of the base had been told by the police that a black soldier had committed murder and rape that day. Since a rifle had been involved, it was decided to check all the carbines issued to the men at the base. While this was being done, Lee Davis arrived in a dishevelled state, with his shoes undone and clothes hastily buttoned up, with some buttons in the wrong buttonholes. He was in an agitated state and declined to say where he had been. None of the rifles had been fired, but one was missing. The missing weapon was not Davis', but anybody could take any of the rifles from the rack where they were stored. After some further investigation, Private Davis was charged with murder and rape, both of which could carry the death penalty.

One recurring feature of the American courts martial at which we are looking is the great rapidity with which matters moved. The murder and rape were committed on 28 September and on 26 October, Lee Davis was sentenced to death. There was a delay of six weeks or so between the sentence being pronounced and carried out. This was to allow the condemned man time to appeal and seek commutation of the sentence. All death sentences had to be confirmed by higher authority in the US Army. It was eventually decided that the 20-year-old soldier should hang on 14 December 1943.

At 1:00 am on the morning of Tuesday, 14 December, Tom Pierrepoint led the young man from the condemned cell to the scaffold, which was only a few yards away. As they entered the execution chamber Lee Davis saw the noose hanging at shoulder height and the full realization of what was about to happen struck him. He faltered for a moment and moaned in a low voice, 'Oh God, I'm going to die!' These were the last words he spoke and after the necessary formalities had been completed, the drop fell and Lee Davis was launched into eternity.

It is difficult to summon up much sympathy for this, the first of the rapists hanged at Shepton Mallet. Davis obviously went out armed with a rifle because he was up to no good and shooting an 18-year-old girl in the back as he did was an appalling crime, as was the rape of Muriel Fawden. He would probably have been hanged in any case, even had he not raped the young woman; the murder of another woman by shooting her in the back would have ensured that.

The rape committed by Madison Thomas, a 23-year-old black soldier stationed in Cornwall, was mundane but brutal. It was the crime of a man overcome with lust, unable or unwilling to restrain himself and with no thought for what the consequences of actions would be, either for himself or his victim.

On the evening of 26 July 1944, Beatrice Reynolds, who lived in the Cornish village of Gunnislake, was walking home after a meeting at the local branch of the Royal British Legion. She was a middle-aged widow, whose husband had been killed during the First World War. She kept house for her brother, who was an invalid. Mrs Reynolds was the Chair of the local British Legion and very active in the community. It was at about 10:30 on what was a very mild evening that she was heading home, when a black American appeared from nowhere and asked her if she had far to go. She did not care for the look of him, so she told him curtly that she did not and carried on walking. Outside one of the houses that they passed, a young woman was sitting. Jean Elizabeth Bright lived with her parents. She knew Mrs Reynolds and they exchanged a few words. By then, it was about eleven o'clock.

Jean Bright later testified that Beatrice Reynolds seemed nervous and acted as though she hoped to shake off the attentions of the young soldier. He disappeared after the two women began talking and when Mrs Reynolds left, she must have thought that she had seen the last of him. Jean Bright recognized the man, for she had seen him pass her house two or three times in the last week or so. When Mrs Reynolds had gone, the man suddenly reappeared and asked Jean Bright if she was going to wish him goodnight. He followed this up by enquiring if she would kiss him, an offer she declined. He then went off down the road at a run in the direction that Beatrice Reynolds had gone.

When the soldier caught up with the woman walking along the lonely road at night, with nobody within earshot or sight, he acted very swiftly and decisively, picking up Mrs Reynolds and putting her over a hedge into a field. Then he scrambled through to join her. By now, it was plain what was on his mind and she pleaded with him to let her go, telling him that she was old enough to be his mother. He replied that this did not matter. He then pulled off a gold watch that Beatrice Reynolds was wearing, telling her that she could have it back when she had given him all that he desired. She said, 'That will never be, boy!' The man then struck her round the head, grabbed her throat and produced a knife. He ripped off her underwear and raped her. After he had finished, he produced a round of ammunition from his pocket and said, 'You see this bullet, if you make any attempt to run, you'll get it!' He then left.

Dr Frederick Woodland came to examine Mrs Reynolds after the attack and saw her in the early hours of 27 July. She had a black eye, a cut on her nose and also severed bruising around her throat. Her vulva was covered in blood and it was Dr Woodland's impression that she had been violently raped and viciously assaulted.

Jean Bright was brought to the Whitchurch Down Camp, the nearby American army base, the following day and the men were all turned out on parade and she walked along the ranks until she was able to identify the man whom she had seen in the company of Beatrice Reynolds. The man she picked out was 23-year-old Madison Thomas. There was more compelling evidence against him though than merely the identification by an eyewitness. When his clothing was examined, it was found that his trousers were bloodstained, a circumstance for which he was unable to provide an explanation. The blood was not of Thomas' group, but matched that of Beatrice Reynolds.

Neither during the investigation nor during his court martial did Thomas make a statement. He exercised his right to silence and it will come as little surprise to learn that he was convicted of rape when his court martial took place on 21 August that year. He was duly convicted and sentenced to death. On 12 October 1944, he was hanged by Tom Pierrepoint, who was assisted by his nephew Albert.

We come now to what is without doubt the worst crime committed by any of the American soldiers who were stationed in the United Kingdom during the Second World War. It is time to meet William Harrison, a man who seemed to lack any redeeming qualities at all. That he had a bad childhood may be true, and the psychiatrists who asserted that he was emotionally deficient and had a psychopathic personality may also be correct, but many people have unsatisfactory upbringings and defective personalities and the overwhelming majority of them do not rape and murder little girls. We may see William Harrison in Illustration 14.

There is something about the sexual abuse and murder of young children that sets such crimes into a class apart. Most of us can find some sympathy with robbers or even with those who murder their husbands or wives. No normal person though can ever hope to understand the thought processes of the man who lures a little girl away from her home so that he can violate and murder her. For this reason, it might be interesting to look at William Harrison's early life before examining the crime for which he was hanged. In this way, we might be able to make some sense of what was, on the face of it, an utterly pointless and wholly unexpected death.

Harrison was born on 27 July 1922 in the town of Ironton, which lies on the bank of the Ohio River. His beginning in life was not auspicious, for his mother was just 14 years of age when she gave birth to him. A consequence of this was that by the time he was a teenager, his uncles and aunts were only in their twenties and not exactly good, mature role models. A number of psychiatrists interviewed William Harrison, after he had been arrested for murder but before he came to trial. Their aim was to establish whether or not he was sane enough to be held to account for his actions.

There is no reason to suppose that William Harrison's childhood was anything other than as represented to the psychiatrists. He said that he started drinking alcohol regularly at 15, while he was still at school. At about the same age, he also enjoyed his first sexual contact with a girl. While at school, his uncle and aunt used to let him get drunk with them. They were, after all, young and irresponsible people themselves. Harrison said that his mother was a secret drinker. Because of the way that he had been raised, it was hypothesised that Harrison had never acquired any moral sense, that is to say, he never learned the difference between right and wrong. He did what he wanted with no regard at all for the consequences. This deficiency in moral sense was, thought one psychiatrist, indicative of a 'constitutional psychopathic personality'. Dr Robert Thompson, a psychiatrist at Armagh's County Mental Hospital, said that William Harrison had never developed any ability to distinguish between right and wrong actions. He said that Harrison genuinely did not know the difference between the sexual act with a child of seven and a prostitute.

There is no doubt that Harrison's record since joining the army was dismal and certainly suggested that he had a serious problem with drinking. By the time that he was arrested for murder and rape in September 1944, he had already been court-martialled five times for being absent without leave due to his heavy drinking. In April 1943 Harrison had been diagnosed as having an inadequate personality, combined with hysteria and amnesia. He had spent six weeks in hospital with amnesia. The most recent of Harrison's courts martial before the final one which signalled the end of his life, was held in June 1944, after he had once again been absent without leave and also deliberately harmed himself. It was thought that he might have done so with a view to being discharged from the army, but in wartime this was not so easy. He was instead sentenced to six months' confinement with hard labour. It was during this last period of imprisonment that Harrison's station commander made a catastrophic error of judgement, which he must later have bitterly regretted. The six months of hard labour should have ended on Boxing Day 1944, but his superior decided to give Harrison one final chance and, in an act of leniency, he ordered his release three months early on 24 September. This set the stage for the tragedy.

On Sunday, 24 September, William Harrison was freed from confinement. It was hoped that he would appreciate this charitable action on the part of his commander and just settle down and behave like the other members of his unit, the 2nd Combat Crew Replacement Center Group, which was based at Clunto Airfield in County Tyrone, Northern Ireland. His response to the commutation of his sentence though was to go on a two-day drinking spree. Some of the men with whom he was serving were also fond of drinking, but they realized that Harrison had a problem in that regard. On the very day that he was released from the guardhouse, Harrison joined a group of men drinking at Dorman's public house in a village near the airfield called Killycolpy. Over the course of four and a half hours, he consumed fifteen beers, each accompanied by a measure of gin, and then finished with two glasses of wine. The following morning, he returned to Dorman's in the late morning and spent most of the day there. By the reckoning of the barman, he drank during this time twenty bottles of beer, eighteen glasses of wine and four or five glasses of stout. It was surprising that he was still able to walk when he left the pub a little before five that afternoon.

In addition to the fellow Americans with whom he drank at Dorman's, William Harrison had also struck up friendships with one or two of the local people in the village, including a man called Patrick Wylie. Patrick Wylie lived in Killycolpy with his wife Mary and their four children. One of these children was 7-year-old Patricia, known to everybody as Patsy. Harrison was on such good terms with the Wylies that he had eaten at their home and even borrowed money from Patrick Wylie. After leaving the pub, the day after he had been released from custody, he went to the Wylies' house to repay the sum of £3 10s (£3.50) which he had borrowed before being locked up for three months.

Patrick Wylie was not at home that afternoon. He had gone fishing, although his wife was there with the children. Harrison expressed his gratitude to her for the friendship which they had shown him and said that he wished to buy them a gift as token of his gratitude. He also offered to fetch some mineral water for the children when he went to the shop. Oddly, he offered to take young Patsy with him to the shops. There was some initial reluctance, but since he was a family friend, it was agreed that Patricia could go with him. It was the last time that the little girl was seen alive. Instead of taking the child to the shops, Harrison led her to a nearby field, where he raped and then strangled her.

Although he made a half-hearted effort to hide the body under some hay, it was soon found and there was no difficulty at all in identifying William Harrison as the man responsible for the dreadful crime. He was arrested almost at once and his court martial took place less than two months later on 18 November. The question to be addressed by the court was not whether or not it was Harrison who had raped and murdered the child; he freely admitted this. The court had to decide if he was responsible for his actions or if his mental state was such that he had diminished responsibility.

A defence of 'diminished responsibility' can be a tricky one, because sometimes the wicked behaviour of a conscienceless psychopath can be mistaken for the actions of an insane person. In William Harrison's case, matters were complicated by the fact that he had been very drunk when he committed the murder and rape, and it is sometimes argued that a very drunk person is incapable of forming the intent which is an essential part of the crime of murder. It was clear that here was a man with no real understanding of what was meant by the terms 'right' and 'wrong', and also that his mind had been addled with drink. Harrison's answers to questions asked of him about what he had done to Patricia Wylie reveal the vacuum which lay at his heart.

Questioned during the court martial, Harrison said that he remembered, 'fooling around' with the child, but could not recall all that happened. When his counsel asked if he had choked Patricia Wylie, he replied that he had. When further asked why he had done so, he answered simply, 'I don't know.' It must be said that his demeanour in court and the way that he gave his evidence had the effect of prejudicing the court against him. The expression, 'fooling around', in contemporary American slang, referred to the kind of preliminary sexual activity in which a man and woman might engage. Hearing the phrase used in connection with a 22-year-old man and little girl of that age gave a terrible impression. Not that anything which William Harrison could say or do in the witness box was likely to affect the ultimate outcome of the trial. None of the men in the court were interested in a lot of fancy talk about amnesia and psychopathic personality disorders. After retiring for just 45 minutes, a verdict of 'guilty' was given and sentence of death pronounced.

There were the usual delays while the sentence was subject to confirmation from above, together with the inevitable appeals for clemency, but it was all in vain. Harrison was sent to Shepton Mallet to await his fate and there, on 7 April 1945, he was hanged by Tom Pierrepoint.

Chapter 8

Three Double Executions

At a little before midnight the night of 4 March 1944, 16-year-old Dorothy Holmes was walking home from a dance held at Bishop's Cleeve in Gloucestershire, not far from the town of Cheltenham. She had gone to the dance with her boyfriend, an American soldier called Edward Hefferman. Passing a public house called the King's Head, the girl noticed two black soldiers standing outside. She observed that after she and her boyfriend had walked a little distance, the two soldiers began to walk after them in the same direction. There were many soldiers about the area though and she thought nothing of it. As they strolled past some fields, the two other men overtook them and one of them struck the man with whom Dorothy was walking a ferocious blow on the head with a bottle. It was sufficient to render him unconscious, whereupon the two of them grabbed the terrified girl and dragged her into a nearby field, where both raped her. Hefferman, when he had recovered his senses, got to his feet and, not seeing the girl he had been with, ran off to try and get help.

Edward Hefferman knocked on the door of the first house to which he came and asked for help, but they had no telephone and advised him to go to the police station. While was looking for the police station, he encountered Dorothy, her clothes in disarray and in great distress. He took her home, where she told her mother that, 'Oh mother, the blacks have had me and they have knocked me about terrible!' She was indeed in a pitiful state. At about 1:00 am a nurse arrived to examine Dorothy, Mabel L. Morehen, and she noted that her lips were bloody and bruised, there were scratches on her legs and both her face and legs, together with her clothes, were muddy.

It was a dreadful crime and the local police were determined that whoever had committed it would not escape justice. When it was light the following morning Detective Sergeant Slade from Cheltenham and Constable Hale of Bishop's Cleeve discovered that there were footprints in the recently fallen snow near the scene of the attack. Taking casts of impressions under such circumstances is a very tricky enterprise, but the two police officers managed to accomplish it and found when they had done so that they had plaster casts of two different boots, both with a distinctive arrangement of nails on the heel. They also took a number of photographs of the prints. The fact that it had been two black men who had carried out the brutal assault strongly suggested that they were American soldiers. Black people were uncommon in that part of England during the Second World War. Because they had no authority to deal with members of the United States forces, the police handed their evidence over to the Military Police based in Cheltenham. Sergeant James Hall of the 255th Military Police Company soon found matches for the casts of the boots in the footwear of two members of the 4090th Quartermaster Service Company. The two men to whom the boots belonged were 25-year-old Eliga Brinson, originally from Tallahassee in Florida, and 22-year-old Willie Smith from Alabama. The name 'Eliga', given for Brinson, is probably a misunderstanding. Sometimes, it is spelled 'Elija' and it is almost certain that his given name was really 'Elijah', after the biblical prophet.

Neither Dorothy Holmes nor Edward Hefferman was able positively to identify either Brinson or Smith, which meant that the case against them would be decided on circumstantial evidence. The first thing which the military police established was that there had been a bed check at 11:30 pm on the night of the assault and neither Eliga Brinson nor Willie Smith were in their bunks. Just to be sure of this, men sleeping near the two suspects were also questioned. Because the offence was such a serious one, nobody felt inclined to provide a false alibi. Private Benjamin Wilkerson, who shared a hut with Brinson, testified that he had been in the hut from 7:30 pm to 11:15 pm on the evening in question and that Eliga Brinson had not been present. Wilkerson had visited the latrine, returning at 11:30 pm, at which time Brinson was still absent. The clothing of both Brinson and Smith was stained with mud on the knees of their trousers and also semen and bloodstains were identified.

Both Eliga Brinson and Willie Smith gave alibis for the evening of 4 March, when the rape had taken place. According to Smith, he had been in Cheltenham that evening, although he was unable to provide any witnesses who saw him there. Brinson admitted having been in two pubs near the base, including the King's Head, but to have left and returned to his bunk before the crime took place. Unfortunately for the two of them, witnesses in their own unit made statements saying that they had seen both men in Bishop's Cleeve on the night in question. One witness put Brinson in the King's Head at about nine that evening, after which he had lost track of him. It seemed fairly certain that both Brinson and Smith had been in Bishop's Cleeve at around the time of the attack.

Then there was the evidence of Dr Edward B. Parks, Director of the Bristol Forensic Laboratory. He had examined the boots of the two accused men and compared them with both the photographs taken and the plaster casts made on the day after Dorothy Holmes was raped. As far as Parks was concerned, the evidence matched up and the footprints made in that field where the assault took place were definitely made by the boots which he had so carefully scrutinised.

Eliga Brinson and Willie Smith were tried by court martial in Cheltenham on 28 and 29 April 1944. Their trial lasted a total of 16 hours and at the end of it there was little to be said in their defence. The two men had, without doubt, attacked a fellow soldier and committed a terrible assault on a helpless young girl. Nobody could have been surprised when the court found them guilty and they were sentenced to death. Neither man had an especially good record. Both had two previous convictions for being absent without leave and Brinson had another conviction by court martial for carrying a concealed knife. The man in overall charge of the US Army in Europe, General Eisenhower, confirmed both the verdict and sentence and on 11 August that year, at one in the morning, the two of them paid the supreme penalty.

Double executions, where two people died side by side, were not an uncommon event in Britain during the first half of the twentieth century. The last time that two men were hanged simultaneously was at London's Pentonville Prison in 1954. The procedure for such executions was more complicated and fraught with hazard than was the case with ordinary hangings. Obviously, with two condemned men, it was important that each was given the correct, carefully calculated, drop. With two nooses and two men, there was of course scope for mishap and the men ending up with the drops meant for each other. To avoid the chance of such an accident, and bearing in mind how small the room containing the gallows usually was, the only practical way of undertaking the execution was to bring in the men one by one. In other words, one of the men would be fetched first from the condemned cell and positioned on the scaffold, with the noose around his neck. Only when this was done would the second man be brought out and led to the gallows. That way, there would be no possibility of any gruesome mishaps such as might result from a man being given too short or too long a drop.

The means by which mistakes in the length of the drop were obviated introduced a new complication. The strain of standing on the scaffold with a rope around one's neck, waiting to die, was immense and it was not unknown for men to faint if left in this position for long. There was also the horrifying shock for the second person to be brought to the scaffold, to be confronted with the sight of somebody standing on the scaffold with a rope already around his neck, waiting to die. As it happened, the execution of Eliga Brinson and Willie Smith went off smoothly, with nobody fainting at the last moment.

It is an uncomfortable fact that six of the executions at Shepton Mallet for rape, and murder and rape, were double hangings. This means that on three separate occasions, pairs of American service personnel conspired together to carry out dreadful attacks on women.

This kind of thing is extraordinarily rare under ordinary circumstances: rapists almost invariable work alone. It was perhaps the peculiar way that single men were sharing barracks in a foreign country which caused this phenomenon. The young, single men crowded together in barracks perhaps encouraged each other in sexual fantasies or exploits. The next case is also that of two men who worked in concert to attack a young girl.

Betty Green's 15th birthday fell on 1 April 1944. That summer, she was therefore just 15½ years old, little more than a child in fact. At that time, most children left school at 14 and found work. Betty, who lived in the Kent town of Ashford, had a job at Norman's Cycle Works. On the evening of 22 August 1944, she walked home from work with her friend Peggy Blaskett, who worked at the same place. Betty arrived home at about 5:45 pm and then, after eating tea, she left the house again at 6:45 to meet up with Peggy Blaskett. The two girls wanted to visit a travelling fair which had been established nearby, in Victoria Park. At the fair, they met two American soldiers with whom they spent the evening. At around 9:45 pm, the girls said goodbye to the men they had met and went home together. They parted at Peggy's home in Frances Road and Betty made her way home from there alone.

As Betty Green made her way home, William Green, her father, was sitting in the Smith's Arms, a public house in Ashford. At about 10:15 pm, Green noticed two American soldiers leaving the pub. He observed that they were the worse for wear, giving every indication that they had been drinking heavily. Betty Green was seen by a railway worker who knew her at about this time. He was cycling home and stopped to speak to her. She was about to walk along a track known locally as the Black Path, which led through some wasteland and fields. An American soldier who had been drinking in the Alfred Arms and was on his way back to his base saw two soldiers walking towards the Black Path at about 10:20.

The two soldiers who had left the Smith's Arms and walked along the Black Path were Corporal Ernest Clark and Private Augustine

Guerra. William Smith later identified them as the men he had seen leaving the pub that night. There was, in any case, no real dispute about this, because Clark and Guerra both made statements in which they admitted to what they had done together after encountering Betty Green. The description which follows is based partly upon their words and also upon the forensic evidence.

As the young girl neared the end of the Black Path, she saw two soldiers walking towards her. One of them, Corporal Clark, asked her where she was going, to which she replied that she was on her way home. It was dark by now and she was in a hurry. Clark asked her if she would go for a walk with him and when she declined, he grabbed her round the waist, picked her up bodily and carried her to a field which lay next to the path. To quote Clarke, once she saw that second man was involved, Betty Green quite justifiably began panicking in earnest; 'She got scared then as Guerra came up and started to holler and Guerra put his hand over her mouth.'

Clarke dragged her further into the field and she began to struggle wildly and to scream. He held her down and put his hand over her mouth to try and keep her quiet, as Guerra lifted her skirt and tore her knickers apart. Guerra pinned one of the girl's arms to the ground and Clark held the other, while also covering her mouth. Guerra then had intercourse with the girl. When he had finished, the two men changed places and Clark got on top of her. To use his own words, as he was 'finishing up on her', he felt Betty Green relax completely and stop struggling. The two men then undressed her further, according to Clark to check for a heartbeat. Having satisfied themselves that the young girl was still alive, they left her in the field and returned to camp.

The following morning, at about 7:15, a man shunting trains on the nearby railway noticed what he thought might be a body laying 20 yards or so from the Black Path. A workmate went to investigate and found the corpse of girl. Judging by the state of her clothes – her underclothes were missing and her dress was rucked up around her waist – he assumed that she had been attacked. When the police were called, they quickly connected the body of a girl with the fact that a girl had been reported to them as not having come home the previous night. William Green was summoned and identified his daughter.

A forensic examination of Betty Green's body showed clearly enough what had befallen her, even before Clark and Guerra had been identified and arrested. Her clothing was torn and there were stains of blood and semen on her and her clothes. Perhaps most significantly of all, there was a large bruise on the right-hand side of her throat, such as could have been made by a thumb, and four smaller bruises on the left, which could have been caused by fingers. There was internal bruising behind the voice-box and the bodily organs showed signs consistent with death from asphyxia. In other words, she had been choked to death.

It did not take long to identify the men whom William Green had seen leaving the pub that night and an examination of their clothing provided all the necessary evidence. Their trousers were, like the dead girl's clothes, stained with semen and blood. Even more damning was the fact that pubic hairs from the men were recovered from the scene of the attack. Faced with such abundant evidence of their guilt, both Clark and Guerra confessed, although claiming that they had not intended to harm the 15-year-old who was on her way home. Clark said during questioning, 'I know I am guilty of the rape but I know I didn't murder her.'

The difficulty which both Clark and Guerra faced was that if you set out deliberately to inflict harm on somebody and that person dies as a consequence of your actions, then unless there are some extremely compelling mitigating circumstances; this is counted as murder. Since the two men admitted setting out to rape Betty Green and she had died in the course of the attack, it is hard to see how the crime could be construed as manslaughter or accidental death.

The two men were tried separately, although both courts martial were held in the same place. Auguste Guerra faced his court martial first, on 22 September 1944. It was convened in Ashford, the town in which Guerra and Clark had committed their crime. Local feeling was running very high about the rape and murder of such a young girl and the wisdom of the stipulation which the Home Office had made when negotiating details of the Visiting Forces Act became clear. That the trial was held in the same town that the crime had taken place allowed local people to see for themselves that there was to be no question of a cover-up and that justice would be seen to be done.

Despite the overwhelming evidence against him, Augustine Guerra chose to plead not guilty to both the charges against him, which were that he had raped and murdered Betty Green. This is the statement which he made to the military police who had investigated the crime. It was read out at his trial.

> It wasn't closing time yet when Corporal Clark and I left the Smith's Arms. It was about 21:45 hours. We both went through the 'Black Path' and noticed a girl on a cycle approaching us in the direction of Smith's Arms', I said hello to her but she didn't answer or stop. At the end or the path to the left, we both saw a girl approaching in our direction. She was a well-built girl, taller than I am. My height is 5 6". I can't recall the description or her clothing. I remained at the corner and Cpl. Clark went after the girl and brought her back to the place where I was standing. I heard Cpl. Clark speak to the girl in the middle of the Railway Bridge. I couldn't hear what was said. I recall that Cpl. Clark had his left arm about the girl's waist. She didn't speak, laugh, cry. I recall now that she said something to the effect of 'Let me go'. Cpl. Clark didn't answer her. He came to me with the girl and said 'Follow me. I did so, walking behind him about 2 or 3 feet to his right. It was dark. He approached the gate, still holding the girl and told me to open the gate. It's a wooden gate leading into a field. Inside the field Clark and the girl went to the left about 50 or 60 feet away against the fence. I was standing beside Cpl. Clark. He laid the girl down on the ground. She didn't move or speak. Clark told me to have

'sexual intercourse' with her first. He asked me if I wanted to 'go on' first. I said 'yes'. I got on top of the girl with my 'fly' of my O.D. trousers unbuttoned. I spread her legs apart and inserted my penis. The girl didn't move, didn't speak, she didn't resist, she didn't kiss me. She was laying on her back. I recall taking her 'panties' off. She was just laying there. I had no trouble about it. Cpl. Clark was standing on the side. I had intercourse with the girl for about 5 minutes. I didn't use a 'rubber'. I know that I discharged inside of her. All this time the girl hadn't spoken a word. She did, I think move her legs. I didn't kiss her. When I arose I saw Cpl. Clark lie down on top of her. I stood aside. I think Cpl. Clark was with her for about 10 minutes. Cpl. Clark didn't use a 'rubber'. I didn't· hear him speak to the girl all this time. I didn't hear her say anything. When Cpl. Clark finished with the girl we both got up and left. The girl remained lying on the ground. She didn't speak or move. We left her lying there. We proceeded back to camp. I don't recall the color of the girl's clothing but I do remember that she had a skirt & a blouse. I know this because I opened her blouse by unbuttoning. The color of it may have been white. As far as I recall I thought that girl was unconscious when I had sexual intercourse with her. Her arms were by her side and I had my hands around her waist. Her eyes were closed. I recall that when we three entered the field, Cpl. Clark had his arms around the girl. I think he lifted her up in both arms and carried her to the spot where we later had intercourse with her. He picked her up by the gate and carried her inside.

After making this appalling statement, which was read out at his court martial, one can only speculate on what Guerra thought that the outcome of his trial might be. He pleaded 'not guilty', but by his own admission had raped a child who had already asked his companion to let her go. After the two of them had finished with her, she was dead.

What did he expect the verdict of the court to be? When judgement was delivered, it can hardly have come as a surprise to the young man who was himself just 20 years of age. The court found Guerra guilty of both rape and murder, saying that;

> It very substantially appears that deceased at no time consented to any of accused's advances. Outside of the written and verbal confession of accused, the evidence convincingly indicates that rape, a felony, was committed by accused, during or shortly after the accomplishment of which act, the victim died of strangulation through manual pressure on her throat applied to stifle her outcries. The accused, if not a principal in that act, was at least an active aider and abettor and under both Federal and military law, equally guilty of her murder.

Augustine Guerra was sentenced to death. When Corporal Clark was himself tried, a short while later on 6 October, the same judgement and verdict were delivered. At one o'clock in the morning of 8 January 1945, Earnest Clark and Augustine Guerra were hanged, side by side, on the gallows of Shepton Mallet Prison.

The next execution to take place at Shepton Mallet was also a double one for rape. Eisenhower could see by the end of 1944 that the war in Europe was drawing to a close. As a result, he wanted all remaining capital cases cleared up as soon as possible, with the process of confirmation of sentence and so on speeded up. This was to ensure that when American forces left Europe, they would not be taking with them any men who had been condemned to death. It was for this reason that the last double execution at Shepton Mallet, which took place on 17 March 1945, was hurried along with breath-taking rapidity. The court martial of the two men who were convicted of the crime took place less than a fortnight after the offence was committed, which showed how keen the Americans were to clear up all outstanding matters in Europe.

At about eight o'clock in the evening on 3 December 1944, Mrs Joyce Broom left her house to visit the local cinema. She lived in at 12 Bonfire Close, in the Somerset town of Chard, which is about 30 miles from Shepton Mallet. On that evening, as she set out to the cinema in Chard, Mrs Broom was more than eight months pregnant and expecting to give birth in a matter of weeks. Soon after leaving her house, the woman became aware that she was being followed. She turned and found two black soldiers who had come up very close to her. One of them said, 'Hello!', to which Mrs Broom replied, 'Hallo, I don't know you and you don't know me.'

When Mrs Broom started to walk off, the two men grabbed hold of her wrists and detained her. She pleaded with them to leave her alone, telling them that she was not only married, but also heavily pregnant. It made no difference to the men, who then began to drag her off. One of them clapped a hand over her face to prevent her from crying out. A scuffle developed as the frightened woman tried to escape and in the ensuing melee, all three of them fell to the ground.

Somehow, the two men managed to drag the woman to a gate leading to an orchard and then succeeded in pulling her into the field. She was still struggling furiously and one or other of the men made sure that her cries could not be heard, by keeping a hand over her mouth. When they felt that they were sufficiently far from the road, Mrs Broom was thrown onto her back and it was obvious to her that they intended to rape her. She begged them to stop and leave her alone, to which, surprisingly, one of the men told her that they loved her. She was then raped by one of the men, while the other restrained her and prevented her from struggling. After the first man had finished, they changed places and the one now holding her down brandished a knife in front of her face.

After the second man had raped her, he stood up and at that moment Joyce Broom managed to snatch the knife. The men, having accomplished their purpose and presumably not wanting to fight for possession of the knife, left. One of them said, 'Don't say anything about this to anyone or we will shoot or kill you!' They told her not to leave the field before they had a chance to get away.

As soon as Mrs Broom reached the road, she encountered a neighbour called Frederick Bandy and told him what had happened. He saw her safely to her home and then went and fetched a policeman from Chard Police Station. Sergeant Arthur Doughty arrived and he in turn sent for a doctor. Dr Albert Glanville examined Mrs Broom immediately and made the following observations. He saw that her lip was bruised and her nose swollen. This was consistent with what she said about having a hand clamped over her mouth. He conducted an intimate examination and found that her vulva was inflamed and that there was semen on her pubic hair and clothes. All three men later testified that the pregnant woman was pale, tearful and agitated.

Some criminal investigations are arduous and drawn-out affairs. Others move so rapidly that, to use a colloquialism, the feet of the perpetrators scarcely touch the ground as they are apprehended and taken into custody. So it was to prove in this case. Company A of the 1698th Engineer Combat Battalion was stationed at Camp Chard and within hours of being informed by the local police of what had happened, they checked the clothing of all the men on the base. That night, the trousers of Corporal Robert Pearson were found to be muddy and wet. The following morning, a pair of trousers belonging to Private Cubia Jones came to light. They too were muddy. Since nobody else's clothes were in that condition, it was only natural that at a little after midday on 4 December, the day after the attack, James E. Connor of the 32nd Military Police Criminal Investigation Section should invite the two men, in the presence of their unit's adjutant, First Lieutenant Albert C. Riggs, to explain how they managed to get into such a state the previous evening. The statements made by the two men were very similar and they freely admitted having intercourse with Joyce Broom, but claimed that it had been consensual.

According to Pearson and Jones, they had met Mrs Broom and Pearson said that they had spoken to her and asked, 'did she care for

1. Thomas Jefferson, the founding father of America, whose policies affected the treatment of American soldiers in Britain during the Second World War.

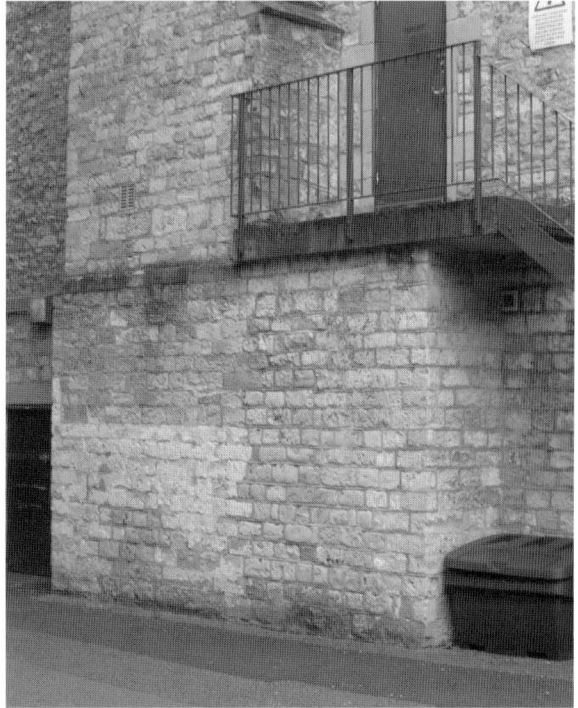

Right: 2. A section of seventeenth-century stonework at Shepton Mallet Prison.

Below: 3. The execution of the conspirators involved in Abraham Lincoln's assassination.

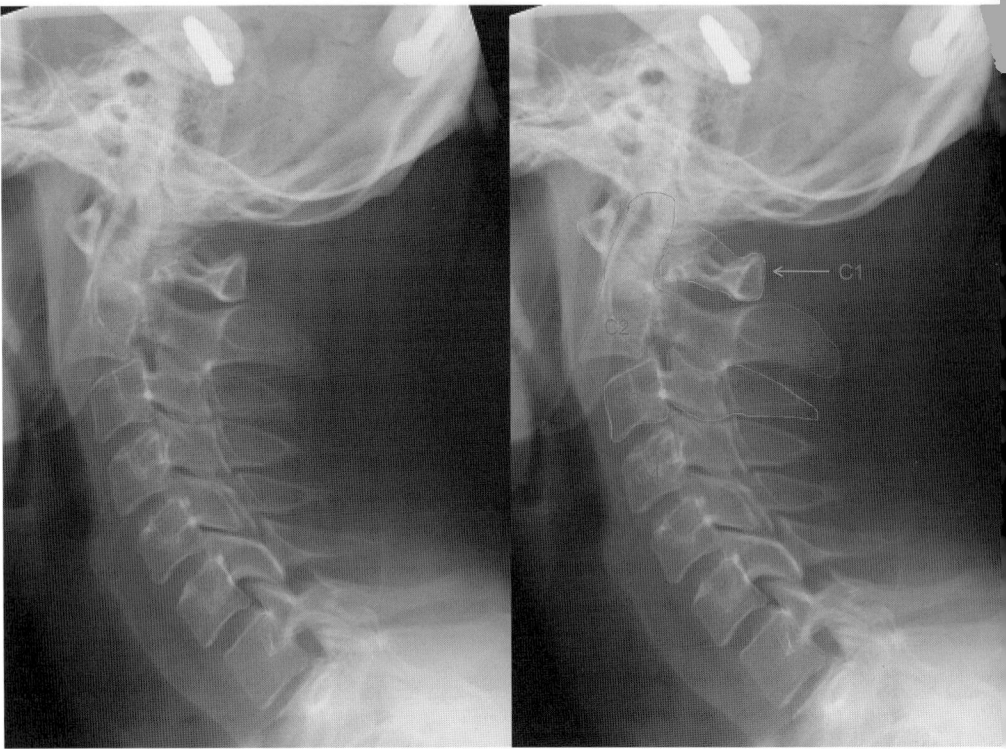

4. An X-ray of the so-called hangman's fracture.

Left: 5. The 'cowboy coil' noose favoured by American executioners.

Below: 6. The free-running noose used in British executions of the twentieth century.

Right: 7. The table of drops used to calculate the distance the prisoner should fall in British executions.

Below left: 8. The new execution building constructed by the Americans when they took over Shepton Mallet Prison in 1942.

Below right: 9. The cramped execution chamber. The railings mark the spot where the trapdoor once was.

...weight of the culprit and his clothing in po[unds] ... [g]ive the length of the drop in feet, but no drop should excee[d] ... [t]hus a person weighing 150 pounds in his clothing will rec[eive] ... [2]000 divided by 150 = 6⅔ feet, *i.e.*, 6 feet 8 inches. The fol[lowing is] [ca]lculated on this basis up to the weight of 200 pounds :—

TABLE OF DROPS.

[W]eight of Prisoner in [hi]s Clothes.	Length of the Drop.		Weight of the Prisoner in his Clothes.	Length of the Drop.		Weight the Priso[ner] his Cloth[es]
	ft.	ins.	lbs.	ft.	ins.	lbs.
[an]d under	8	6	138 and under	7	3	167 and u[nder]
,,	8	5	140 ,,	7	2	169 ,,
,,	8	4	141 ,,	7	1	171 ,,
,,	8	3	143 ,,	7	0	174 ,,
,,	8	2	145 ,,	6	11	176 ,,
,,	8	1	146 ,,	6	10	179 ,,
,,	8	0	148 ,,	6	9	182 ,,
,,	7	11	150 ,,	6	8	185 ,,
,,	7	10	152 ,,	6	7	188 ,,
,,	7	9	154 ,,	6	6	190 ,,
,,	7	8	156 ,,	6	5	194 ,,
,,	7	7	158 ,,	6	4	197 ,,
,,	7	6	160 ,,	6	3	200 ,,
,,	7	5	162 ,,	6	2	
,,	7	4	164 ,,	6	1	

When for any special reason, such as a diseased condi[tion of] the culprit, the Governor and Medical Officer think that [a] departure from this table, they may inform the executio[ner] [...]n as to the length of the drop which should be given in tha[t case]

10. The remains of the trapdoors' hinges are still visible on the rafters below the modern floorboards.

11. Thomas Pierrepoint. By the time he undertook the execution of the American soldiers, he was in his seventies.

Right: 12. Albert Pierrepoint. Thomas Pierrepoint's nephew and his assistant at most of the hangings carried out at Shepton Mallet.

Below left: 13. Lee Davis was the first man to be executed for rape in Britain for over a century.

Below right: 14. William Harrison committed one of the worst crimes seen in Britain during the Second World War.

MILITARY POLICE
IV TPMO ETO
O 919

Death Sentence for Attack On Bath Woman

COURT-MARTIAL ON COLOURED SOLDIER

"HE held a knife over me," declared a Combe Down woman at a court martial at a United States Army Camp in the West Country on Thursday, when a coloured soldier was found guilty of rape and sentenced to be hanged.

The Court included one coloured member. Captain Cullison prosecuted, and Major Drew defended the accused, who pleaded not guilty. A colonel presided over the Court, which consisted of eight officers.

The woman said: "I am a house-wife and don't know the accused. I can't say I can see him in this

the Avenue heard someone coming at speed. He found it was his wife.

Witness said: "I said, 'What-ever is the matter?' My wife said: 'Oh, he has got a knife.' I said: 'Where is he?' as I wanted to make after him. My wife said: 'Don't go. He will stab you with that knife.'

"She said the man had assaulted her. She was nearly collapsing. so he took her to the Aid Post."

On the way to see the doctor his wife gave out a scream. She said:

Councill
MA.
BATH
TO
The circ
ties by Mr.
Secretary
Security,
who are
Defence a
tion, will
Wednesda
Civil Defe
There is
local City
has to be
the new gi
ment. He
City Coun
the Civil
is also Chi
His dual
paragraph
states:
"Membe
occupying
sibility ir
dinate to

15. A newspaper article about the court martial of Leroy Henry.

16. The wall in Shepton Mallet Prison where two men were executed by firing squad.

Right: 17. Sir Eric Teichman, the British diplomat who died when he went to investigate a suspected poacher.

Below: 18. Honingham Hall, the palatial home of Sir Eric Teichman at the time of his murder.

Left: 19. Master-Sergeant John C. Woods, the American Army's executioner in Europe.

Below: 20. Plot E at the Oise-Aisne Cemetery and memorial in France, where the bodies of the soldiers executed at Shepton Mallet now lie.

any company and she said that we do not know her'. Following which exchange, Pearson said that he and Jones had each taken one of her arms and they had led her to the field, where she willingly had intercourse with both of them. He denied having a knife or even seeing one. Jones, in his statement, said much the same, except that he admitted that he had had a knife but misplaced it.

The court martial of Robert Pearson and Cubia Jones was held at Chard on 16 December and the two men placed all their hopes, slender as they were, on their claim that Joyce Broom had been a willing participant in the sexual acts. It was even claimed that she had hugged and kissed the men while having intercourse with her. Jones was 24 at the time of his trial, while Robert Pearson was just 21 years of age.

The defence did not have an easy time, but they did the best with what little material there was. When Frederick Bandy was called to give evidence of what Joyce Broom said to him when he first met her that night, defence counsel objected to him as a witness 'on the grounds of remoteness and hear-say', a suggestion which was at once dismissed, by the court. There was also an attempted to try and have deleted from Pearson's statement anything mentioning Jones and vice versa. This request too was denied, although the court ruled that 'the statement Jones made concerning Pearson shall not be considered against Pearson and the statement Pearson made or reference he made concerning Jones shall not be considered against Jones'.

The two men, by their own admissions, had had sex with Joyce Broom. The only question to determine was whether or not she had consented to the act. Her bruised lip, swollen nose and general demeanour a very short while after the act militated strongly against any idea that she had been a willing party to what occurred. The fact that she had snatched a knife from one of the two men was also indicative that threats as well as violence had been involved. It did not take the court long to find both men guilty of rape, contrary to the 92nd Article of War. It remained only to decide if the sentence should be life imprisonment or death. That the victim had been heavily pregnant weighed against Pearson and Jones. In the end, the court could find no mitigating circumstances whatsoever and the two of them were sentenced to be hanged.

At one o'clock in the morning of Saturday, 17 March 1945, Robert Pearson and Cubia Jones met for the last time on the scaffold of Shepton Mallet Prison, where they had been detained since the court martial. They had to wait twice as long, standing on the trapdoor contemplating their imminent death, as did an individual being hanged on the gallows there. This was because the awful process of reading out the charge, explaining the verdict of the court martial and going through all the rigmarole of setting out the steps by which the sentence had been confirmed, had to be carried out twice, as did the enquiry as to whether the men had any last statement to make before they died. Then it was time for Tom Pierrepoint to place the white hoods over their heads and the ropes around their necks. He was assisted on the occasion of this, the last double execution to take place at Shepton Mallet, not by his nephew but instead by a man called Herbert Morris.

Chapter 9

The Rapist Who Never Was

Despite the endemic racism which was so entrenched within the army of the United States during the Second World War, there was an occasional and heartening flash of common sense and humanity. One such case involved a supposed case of rape and brought an innocent man within a few yards of the gallows. Fortunately, in this instance, the inexorable course of events which often transported black men to their death at the hands of an executioner was derailed at the last moment.

There was a general assumption by American courts, both civil and military, that there was something unsavoury, and often criminal, in any sexual contact between black men and white women. This perception, common enough in the United States, was brought to Britain and influenced the way that cases of rape were dealt with by American courts martial.

In 1943 Leroy Henry, a black man, was called up and conscripted into the US Army. He was assigned to the 3914th Quartermaster Gasoline Supply Company, which was responsible for supplying petrol to various army units. In 1944 Corporal Henry was stationed in England, as preparations gathered pace for the invasion of Europe, which took place in June of that year. Because the supply of fuel was of crucial importance to the Normandy landings, it is very likely that Leroy Henry would have been sent across the English Channel to France when D-Day arrived, but instead the 30-year-old soldier found himself on trial for his life. He was charged with rape, which of course put him in hazard of his life. The story of the supposed crime was a strange one.

According to the evidence presented to the court martial, held in the Wiltshire town of Warminster, Henry's offence could hardly have been more straightforward. At 11:20 on the night of 5 May 1944 a married couple living in a cottage in Combe Down, a village on the outskirts of Bath, were awakened by tapping on a downstairs window. They were in bed at the time, in an upstairs room. The sequence of events which followed sounds more than a little peculiar to an unbiased observer. The account which follows is taken directly from the transcripts of the court martial which took place three weeks later.

According to 33-year-old Mrs Irene Lilley, who lived in the cottage with her husband and two children, 'I got out of bed and looked out of the window. I could see a coloured soldier standing by the wall below. I said, "Do you want anything?" He said, "Yes, I am lost. I have come to find my brother. I found he is not there, I have to get back to Bristol tonight. Could you tell me of any transport or buses to get me there?"'

After a some more conversation, Mrs Lilley went downstairs to invite the soldier into her house, so that she could write down directions for him to get to the nearest railway station. As she remarked to her husband before doing so, 'A coloured soldier outside wants me to go down and write down directions to the station. I think I had better do it.'

The upshot of all this, according to Irene Lilley's recollection, was that she then offered to show the soldier the way to the station and went off into the night with him, wearing only her nightclothes. She told the court martial that she had 'got dressed', but then admitted that this simply meant putting on her knickers. During all this, her husband lay incuriously in bed, and did not contribute anything to the exchanges.

Already, the story told sounds a little odd. Why on earth should Leroy Henry rouse a couple in this way in the middle of the night and whatever possessed the woman, who was a few years older than the soldier, to go off with him like that? We shall shortly see Corporal Henry's explanation of what was going on and be able to compare it with that of Mrs Lilley.

Irene Lilley's husband said that he became uneasy when his wife did not return after a short time and went off in search of her. He came across her laying in a ditch. She claimed that the man who she had been helping had raped her, after threatening her with a knife. The police were called and as they were driving Irene Lilley to a doctor, the man who had tapped on the window of the Lilley's house was seen walking along the road. The local police arrested him and later handed him over to American Military Police. He confessed to having raped the woman and three weeks later faced a court martial, in the course of which he was found guilty and sentenced to death. Leroy Henry was then removed to Shepton Mallet Prison, to wait for his appointment with the hangman.

This briefly is the case which according to one historian became the most publicized and discussed incident relating to the American forces stationed in the United Kingdom. On the face of it, it looks a fairly clear case of rape and whatever we might think about the idea of executing a man in Britain for something which had not been a capital crime in that country for a century, we would most of us think that Leroy Henry was likely to be guilty of the offence with which he had been charged. It is time to look at the business not only from Henry's side, but also from that of the 33,000 local people who signed a petition calling for a reprieve.

The confession which was read out in court sounded damning enough, but Leroy Henry claimed that he had been mistreated and threatened by the Military Police into making it. During the trial, Irene Lilley had told the court that she had never set eyes on Henry before in her life and that he was a complete stranger. The accused man though said that he had had sex with her twice before, each time paying her £1, equivalent at that time to about £50 today. He went on to explain to the court that there was a more-or-less a standing arrangement that if a soldier went to visit Mrs Lilley, she would have sex with the man for money. In short, he suggested that the housewife was a part-time prostitute.

According to Leroy Henry, what had actually happened on that May night was that Mrs Lilley had gone off with him, wearing only her nightclothes, on the understanding that she would have intercourse with the soldier for money. They had previously agreed that he would come to the house on the evening of 5 May. In his words;

> She told me to knock at a certain window. I knocked and she stuck her head out of the window. I heard her talking to somebody. She rushed downstairs and invited me in. When I heard somebody moving about, I asked where Bristol was. When I walked out the door, she followed behind. I went into a field. We had been there a couple of times before. I assisted her over the wall. She asked me for £2. I did not have £2, but I told her I had well over £1. She walked off and said, 'I will get you into trouble!' I laughed and walked on.

Before relinquishing all authority over American soldiers stationed in their country, the British government had been clear that men charged with serious offences such as murder and rape should be tried as close as possible to the place where the crimes were allegedly committed. It was also thought desirable that such trials be reported in the British press, so that there would be no suspicion that an American court martial had allowed one of their own soldiers to get away with murder. This openness turned out, at least in the case of Leroy Henry, to be a double-edged sword. In most parts of the United States, the trial and conviction of a black man charged with raping a white woman would generally have been a fairly swift business, with the verdict seldom being in doubt, even before the evidence had been heard. Britain, though, was a different place entirely and the citizens of Bristol and Bath were not as ready as the Americans to make assumptions about people based solely on the colour of their skins.

There were, to the British public in the West Country, a number of disturbing aspects of the death sentence passed on Corporal Henry. The fact that rape was not, and had not been for a hundred years, a capital crime in Britain was one thing which stood out. Another was the extraordinary speed of the judicial process leading to Henry's being despatched to the condemned cell. The events which formed the basis for the prosecution took place on the night of 5 May. By 25 May, less than three weeks later, he had been sentenced to death. By any standards, that was very swift work indeed.

There was another point which aroused public sympathy for the condemned man and that was the fact that he was black. There was no tradition in Britain of what was known as a 'colour bar' and the great majority of people saw the black soldiers as Americans, rather than being black or white. It was quite noticeable during American courts martial held in Britain at that time for offences involving the civilian population, that the American officers, whether prosecuting or defending, usually referred to the colour of black soldiers. They might talk of the 'negro', for instance. British witnesses at such proceedings hardly ever did so. They spoke instead of 'the American' or 'the soldier'.

It did not take long after the arrival of American forces in Britain before people observed that the army was segregated by race into black and white units and that black soldiers appeared surprised to be allowed to visit the same shops and bars as white people. This gave an unfavourable impression to many people of American culture and black soldiers found themselves the object of sympathy for the way in which they were treated by their own countrymen.

There was another way in which the reports of the court martial which appeared in local papers, such as the *Bath Chronicle and Weekly Gazette*, raised a few eyebrows. Irene Lilley's evidence of going off at midnight in her nightie to show an unknown soldier the way to the railway station might have been an act of selfless altruism, but there can be no doubt that it was an odd story. Corporal Henry's tale, on the other hand, had for many readers a ring of truth about it. Although it is seldom mentioned today, there was a good deal of casual prostitution in areas where the American forces were stationed. The soldiers had money and also various foodstuffs and luxury items which were sorely lacking in wartime Britain. The idea that a housewife in Bath had been supplementing the housekeeping money by having sex with American soldiers for £1 a time was perfectly plausible. In sort, quite a few readers of papers like the *Bath Chronicle and Weekly Gazette* felt that the young soldier had received a raw deal and a campaign was started to secure a reprieve for him.

Foremost in the efforts to save Leroy Henry's life was a local baker called Jack Allen. Appalled at what seemed to him an obvious miscarriage of justice, he began a petition calling for Henry to be reprieved. Allen was a determined man and his initial plan of collecting signatures soon snowballed into something bigger. Sam Day, a magistrate in Bath, joined him in organizing an effective campaign which saw 33,000 people sign the petition. National newspapers took an interest in the case and serious question began to be asked about the quality of the legal process at Corporal Henry's court martial. The D-Day landings were due to begin on 6 June and if ever there was a time that unity was required between Britain and America, it was in the days leading up to the invasion. The Allied Supreme Commander General Eisenhower, later of course to become President of the United States, was appalled at what was happening at such a crucial juncture in the war. There can be little doubt that Eisenhower would have known that this kind of railroading of a black man accused of raping a white woman was by no means unusual in the United States. It was, however, plain that what might be tolerated in Alabama or Georgia would not be acceptable to the people living in Somerset.

Eisenhower was famed for his decisiveness. On this occasion he refused in the first instance to confirm the sentence of death passed and set aside the finding of guilt. At this point, he could have ordered a retrial, but probably wanted to be rid of such a vexing distraction once and for all. He declared the case closed and ordered Leroy Henry to be freed and returned to his unit without a stain on his character. The unit in which Henry served was after all vital to the ability of the US Army to advance from the landing beaches in Normandy. The drivers of the fuel trucks were almost all black and in some ways their role was more important than the ordinary infantryman. As General Patton famously remarked, 'My men can eat their belts, but my tanks have gotta have gas.'

What was the truth of the matter about that May evening almost 80 years ago? Was a woman brutally raped or did an angry prostitute who felt cheated out of £2 decide to be revenged upon the man whom she felt to be a cheapskate and timewaster? It is impossible after all these years to be sure, but there can be little doubt that it would be very unwise to convict anybody on the available evidence. Perhaps the best verdict would be the old Scottish one of 'Not Proven'.

Chapter 10

A Collection of Murderers

H aving looked at some of those who were hanged at Shepton Mallet Prison for rape, sometimes accompanied by murder, we turn now to those executed for murder alone. We saw that David Cobb, the first man to be executed at Shepton Mallet, was hanged for murdering another soldier on an army base. The next execution at the prison while it was under American control was for a similar crime. There can have been few more pointless murders than that committed by Private Harold A. Smith on 9 January 1943.

On New Year's Eve 1942, Harold Smith was detained in the guardhouse at Chiseldon Camp near the Wiltshire town of Swindon. He belonged to the 1st Tank Destroyer Group. With him in detention was Harry English of the 984th Tank Destroyer Battalion. Everybody else was making merry and celebrating, which perhaps caused the two young men to feel left out. Whatever the reason, they broke out of the guardhouse and headed for London.

For a week Harold Smith and Harry English enjoyed all that London had to offer. All things come to an end though and they eventually ran out of money. On 8 January, a week after he had gone off on his jaunt, Smith returned to Chiseldon Camp to collect some money which he said was owed to him, only to find that his unit had been sent elsewhere. This was something of an unexpected complication and rather than tackle the problem head on, Harold Smith procrastinated and spent the night at the camp without drawing too much attention to himself. By ill chance, he found a loaded 0.45 pistol laying around, at least according to his own account. The guards coming off duty used to just leave their pistols laying around. The statement which he

later made tells us what next happened and also contains an account
of his time in London;

I, Private Harry Adolphus Smith, ·ASM 14045090, Hq.
Hq.Co. 1st Tank Destroyer Group, APO #302 having been
duly warned do hereby make the following statement, entirely
of my own free will without threat or promise of reward. At
about 5:00 P.M. on Friday, Jan 1st 1943 I went A.W.O.L. from
my unit and went to London. I had just been paid and had
about £5. I rented a room at the Royal Hotel, Russell Square,
London. Private Harry English, 894th Tank Destroyer Bn.
whom I met on the train coming to London, also stayed in
my room, #5077, at the Royal Hotel. He was also A.W.O.L.
from his outfit. On the following day, Saturday, I went around
London, sightseeing and going to the movies. Private English
was with me for a short while. He later left to meet a girlfriend.
I do not know her name but I recall that she was in room
#2053 at the Royal Hotel. On Saturday night, Jan 2nd, English
engaged room #1001 at the Royal Hotel. We both stayed in
that room. English and I kept room #1001 until Thursday,
Jan. 7th 1943. I did not see much of English as he was with his
girlfriend most of the time. At about 3:30 P.M., on Thursday,
English introduced me to a British Merchant seaman who
invited us to his home. His name was Pete. I do not know his
address as we went to his house by taxi. English and I both
stayed at Pete's house for the night. At about 1:00 P.M. on
Friday, Jan. 8th 1943, English and I left Pete's house. English
went to Victoria and I went to Paddington Station to get a
train and return to my unit. English had a date with a girl
in Victoria. He told me he would meet me in Swindon the
following day. I caught the 9:20 P.M. train from Paddington
Station, Friday night. I arrived in Swindon at about 11:45 the

same night. I immediately went to Chilsedon camp, 6 miles from Swindon, to rejoin my unit. I found my organization had moved out. I saw a light in one of the camp kitchens so I entered and asked for something to eat. A guard, armed with a pistol, was on duty in the kitchen. There was no cook around so the guard gave me a cheese sandwich. He grumbled quite a bit about me asking for something to eat after hours. Another guard who was present in the kitchen went to the barracks and made arrangements for me to sleep there. I, and the guard who gave me the sandwich, followed the other guard to the barracks. I slept there in a bunk pointed out by the guard who had gone ahead to make arrangements. I got up the next morning at about 7:00 A.M. I did not eat any breakfast. (I very seldom eat breakfast) I hung around the barracks until about noon when I went to the mess hall for dinner. After dinner I went back to the squad room where I had slept. At about 2:00 P.M. that day, Saturday, Jan. 9th 1943, while in the squad room I saw a U.S. Army .45 cal. Automatic pistol, holster, web belt and 3 full clips of ammunition. The pistol was laying on top of a bunk. I strapped the belt and pistol around my blouse, under my overcoat, and walked out of the barracks, at about 4:00 P.M. While in the corridor I checked the clip in the pistol. Finding it was full I pushed it back in the pistol. I always wanted to have an automatic so I took the gun from the squad room intending to keep it as a souvenir. I had no intention of using the gun or shooting anybody. After checking the clip in the corridor, I started walking toward the mess hall. Just as I got outside the barracks I met a guard armed with a pistol. He looked like the guard who had given me the sandwich in the kitchen. the night before. When I was about six feet away from the guard I said to him 'Hiya Bud' When I got about even with him and just as we were passing each other, the guard turned to me and said, 'What the hell did you say?' I stopped and replied 'I just said hiya Bud'. The guard said 'What do you mean by that?' I replied 'Just Hiya Bud.' When I said that the guard took a step toward me and at the same time bringing his right hand back toward his holster. I did not know whether he was going to hit me or draw his pistol and shoot me. At this time the guard and I were about four feet from each other. As the guard made the motion toward his holster I immediately drew my pistol from under my unbuttoned overcoat with my right hand. All in the same motion I pumped a cartridge into the chamber with my left hand and fired point blank at the guard's stomach from the hip position. When the first shot hit the guard he spun around to the right until his back was toward me. I then fired one or more shots (I can't remember the number) into the guard's back. As I was shooting the guard was falling to the ground. After I had finished firing at the guard at my feet, I remained there for a few moments standing over him with the pistol still in my hand. At this time I saw an unarmed soldier come out of the barracks and run toward me with clenched fists. I fired two shots over his head to scare him. He turned around and ran back into the barracks. I then holstered my pistol and ran away from the scene of the shooting. I ran out of the camp, along the Ogburne – Marlborough road. I caught a bus at Ogburne at about 4:30 P.M. and went to Marlborough, about four miles away. I arrived at Marlborough at about 5:00 P.M. on Jan. 9th 1943, the day of the shooting. I remained around Marlborough until about midnight at which time I caught a train for London. I arrived at Paddington Station, London, at about 4:00 A.M. Sunday, Jan. 10th 1943. As the tubes were closed I took a taxi and went to Euston Station where I sat in a chair at the Y.M.C.A. Restrooms. Sunday morning at about 8:00 A.M., Private English came to the Restrooms. We talked a while and I told him my outfit had moved. I did not tell him anything about me shooting a guard in Chisledon. I did however show him the pistol I was carrying. He asked me to loan it to him. I did so at about 8:05 A.M. He went out with the pistol and returned about 15 minutes later gave it back to me. English then left me saying he would meet me in the Restrooms that night. After English left I also went out of the Restrooms and walked around London. I returned to the Y.M.C.A. at Euston Station late Sunday afternoon and remained there. I slept in one of the chairs. At about 2:30 A.M. on Monday Jan 11th 1943 I was awakened by a uniformed London Policeman. He took my pistol away from me and escorted me to a police station. I was later turned over to the U.S. Military Police and put in jail. I know the number of the pistol I stole from the barracks in Chisledon and which I used in shooting the guard is 515525. I have memorized this number. I drank no liquor on the day of the shooting. I have read my-statement of 9 pages and 6 lines and it is all true. (Signed) Harold Adolphus Smith.

This chilling account gives no reasonable explanation as to why Smith shot the man who approached him. The man concerned, Harry Jenkins, lost so much blood that he died that same day. The following day Harold Smith was picked up by the police in London and handed over to the American Military Police, who charged him with murder. In due course, he appeared before a court martial in Bristol on 12 March 1943.

Smith had made a statement after being arrested in which he admitted shooting Harry Jenkins and there was nothing which the officer defending him could do. The defence tried various gambits, for example claiming that Harold Smith was really only 16 years old at the time of the murder. In fact, he was 20. In the end, there was little to be done, other than plead for mercy, in other words a sentence of life imprisonment rather than death. It was a hopeless cause and so, after the usual procedure of appealing and the sentence being confirmed, Harold Smith was hanged at Shepton Mallet on 26 June 1943.

The next man to be executed for murder after an American court martial was considerably older than those at whom we have so far looked. They were in their early twenties, but he was almost 40 years old. He was of an age at which most men have settled down sufficiently that they are not likely to become involved in crimes of passion.

RAF Medmenham in Buckinghamshire was of crucial importance in attempts to mitigate the effect of the ballistic missiles launched at Britain in the closing years of the Second World War. Aerial reconnaissance had shown that something strange was happening in parts of occupied Europe and the suspicion grew that some new weapon was being developed by the Nazis. Ordinary photographs were not able to show clearly enough what was happening at sites such as Peenemünde in the Baltic and so stereoscopic images were taken by specially-adapted aircraft. Some of these were then turned into realistic models. The purpose was that if, as seemed likely, it would be necessary at some time to bomb these sites, the models would be used for training the aircrews of the bombers. The Americans were heavily involved in this process and one of their best model-makers was Private John H. Waters, aged 38 in 1943.

While stationed in Buckinghamshire, Waters was carrying on affair with a woman living a few miles away in the town of Henley-upon-Thames. Doris Staples, who was 35, had what was once known as an 'understanding' with an American soldier who had been posted to North Africa as part of the planned invasion of Sicily which began on 9 July 1943. While he was away though, she picked up with John Waters. She evidently found American service personnel to her taste, because by all accounts he was not the only American soldier with whom she was associating. Perhaps she felt that at her age and social position, marriage to an American might rescue her from a life which was singularly lacking in romance and excitement. She was, after all, single and fast approaching middle age. Her job too was a mundane one; she worked in a draper's shop in Henley.

There was tension in Doris Staples' relationship with John Waters and much of it centred around her intentions towards the other American soldier with whom she was involved. Matters reached a head on 14 July 1943, when John Waters walked out of RAF Medmenham without permission and when he was supposed to be on guard duty, and went to the draper's shop in Henley where his girlfriend worked, to confront her over her relationship with the other men in her life. Unfortunately for all involved, he had with him a loaded revolver which had been issued to him when he went on duty.

He first went to the shop where his supposed girlfriend worked at lunchtime, when she was not there. He returned at about 2:30 pm and spoke a few words to Doris Staples. Two other women who worked in the draper's shop testified subsequently that Doris Staples was very freely affectionate with American soldiers and that she did not wish to be tied down to one man. It seems clear that she was trying to get rid of John Waters and was beginning to view him as something of a nuisance. At 4:30 pm, there was a tap on the window of the shop and one of the women who worked there remarked, 'He's here again!' Doris Staples replied, 'What does he want now? I had better go out and see what he wants.' She did so and held a brief conversation with the man, saying at one point, 'I can't come out with you now Johnny, I'm working'. The owner of the shop, Izzy Aaronson, told her to stop gossiping and get back to work.

Events now moved very swiftly to a tragic climax. As the woman went back into the shop, she attempted to close the door behind her, but Waters put out his foot to prevent her doing so. He entered the shop after Doris Staples and pulled out the pistol which he was wearing on a lanyard around his neck. He then fired three shots, whereupon the woman fell to the floor. Gertrude Hurst, who also worked there, thought that her friend had fainted and went to fetch some water to revive her. Far from fainting though, Doris Staples had actually sustained three bullet wounds. He fired twice more at the prone figure. Rebecca Woolf, the other woman working that day in the shop, then witnessed the horrifying sequel to the murder. She said that he 'twisted the revolver round' and then said, 'Not you Betty!' As she watched, the American put the muzzle of the pistol beneath his chin and fired once. He then collapsed.

It is hardly surprising that those working in the shop fled in terror. One of the woman who ran shrieking from the shop told a passer-by what had happened and he seized a bicycle leaning against a wall and raced to the police station to sound the alarm. Inspector Henry Morris, from Henley, arrived at about 4:45 pm to find a group of people surrounding the draper's shop. One of them called out that there was a man inside who was armed. As the inspector was considering his options, two soldiers arrived from the base where Waters was stationed. Captain Harrison Reed and Sergeant Cloud offered to deal with the situation, which the British police officer was glad to allow them to do. Captain Reed shouted, 'Are you all right Johnny? Throw out your gun.' There was no reply and so the captain, who had come equipped for any eventuality, threw a tear-gas grenade through the door of the shop.

Any hope that this would put an end to what seemed to be developing into a siege were dashed when somebody in the crowd called to the Americans, 'He's just moved!' A moment later, two shots rang out. One smashed a window on the other side of the road and the other ricocheted off the surface of the road, sending the crowd diving for cover. Somebody thought that he had seen the man in the shop get up and move into the yard at the back. Showing tremendous bravery, Captain Reed and Sergeant Cloud went through the fish shop which adjoined the shop where the shooting had taken place and made their way through to the backyard of this shop, which was separated from the yard at the back of the draper's shop by only a fence. The two of them clambered over the fence and found John Waters slumped in an outside toilet, bleeding heavily from a wound to his jaw. After he was disarmed, Captain Reed noted that his breath smelt strongly of alcohol.

Although the general pattern in such cases as this was to arrange a court martial as soon as was humanly possible, this proved impractical in this instance because Waters was so gravely injured. He defied all expectations and clung on to life and it was not until November that he was thought by doctors to be well enough to go on trial. The court martial was held in Watford on the 29th of the month.

Five days after all the murder, while he was still being treated in hospital, John Waters made the following statement.

> STATEMENT OF John Henry Waters DATED 19 July 1943 TAKEN BY Agent Edmund P. Crovo: Place: Ward 7, 2nd General Hospital APO 647, it is my duty to inform you of your rights at this time. It is your privilege to remain silent. Anything you say may be used either for or against you in the event that this investigation results in a trial. Do you thoroughly understand. your rights? SIGNATURE: John H. Waters STATEMENT: I am a patient at the 2nd General Hospital. I am 36 years old. I met Doris last February. I saw her nearly every day. I used to go to see her at the dress shop where she worked. I used to take her to movies and to pubs. On last Tuesday I was with Doris and we had an argument. We argued because she was stepping out and it made a god dam fool of me. Henley is a small town and everyone knows the others business. I didn't like her stepping out. On last Wednesday the 14th of July I went down to see Doris at her work early in the morning. She was not in so I went back to camp. I messed around camp for a while and I was burned up at Doris. I went on guard duty and left my post and rode a bicycle up to where she works. I gave her a picture of herself that she had given me some time before. We talked for a while and then she went in the store. I was standing just inside the store and I pulled the cannon and shot her. I don't know where or how many times. She fell down and then I shot myself. I don't remember what the hell, went on afterwards I would only be guessing if I told you. She was going with a fellow who is now in Africa. He was

a married man and didn't get along with his wife but got along with her. I think she was in love with him. I shot her because I don't like any pushing around. She used me to get something for herself. I used to give her a lot of little gifts. She used tell me she had to go home early and the boys would see her later in the evening with another guy. That burned me up. I had never thought of shooting her. I had intercourse with her on numerous occasions. Once she told me she was pregnant and I gave her money to straighten it out. I used to think she was having intercourse with other guys and when I thought of it I got burned up. I was afraid she would turn me down in favor of the others. If she went out with others and was a lady about it and told me I wouldn't have minded but I don't like this lying stuff I am a married man with one child. I have read my statement of 3 pages and it is true. SIGNED: John H, Waters.

That the US Army was very annoyed with all the public trouble which Waters had brought is evident by the charges which he eventually faced when once he had sufficiently recovered his health. Not only was he charged with murder, but also with wounding himself, which was a breach of the Articles of War and also even with leaving the guard duty without authorization. There was very little that Waters could say in defence of his actions, other than to represent it as a crime of passion. In other words, his emotions had reached such a pitch that he was not really answerable for his actions. This was unlikely to work, not least because the whole affair had been a hideous embarrassment for the Americans. It was exactly the kind of bad publicity which they did not want for their armed forces at that time, with preparations being made for the invasion of Europe and unity between them and their British allies being of paramount importance. When the sentence of death came, it was no more than anybody had expected.

It was to be three months before John Waters stood on the scaffold at Shepton Mallet and it is interesting to note that had he been sentenced by a British court, he would almost certainly have been reprieved. This is not because there were any mitigating circumstances to the case – there were none – but due to a purely mechanical factor. When condemned men had previously attempted suicide in a manner which damaged their neck or jaw, it was usual in Britain not to hang them. The reason was simple, a large and recently healed gash in the throat might open up under the impact of the drop, causing a lot of blood to flow or even, in a worst-case scenario, decapitation. With injuries to the jaw, things could be even worse, because judicial hanging as practised in Britain entailed the rope jerking the head back, by exerting sudden and immense pressure of the jaw. This had the effect of levering back the head and snapping the spinal cord. John Waters' jaw had been shattered and fixed back together in hospital. If it gave way under the strain of being hanged, then the rope could actually slip over his head and he would then fall to the ground. This was a ghastly prospect. However, the Americans were determined to go ahead and in the event, the execution passed off without incident. On 10 February 1944 Tom Pierrepoint, this time assisted not by his nephew Albert but by a man called Alex Riley, hanged John Waters at one in the morning.

The next execution of a murderer at Shepton Mallet is perhaps unique in British criminal history in that two men, strangers to the extent that one did not even know the name of the other, committed a murder together. It is also unusual in that both the men accused of the murder were tried simultaneously, but in separate courtrooms. The story concerns two black soldiers who, like Harold Smith at whom we looked at the beginning of this chapter, could bear rural life no longer and wished to visit London. The first of these men was a sergeant called George Fowler and he took a trip to London at the start of December 1943, overstaying by two days the leave to which he was entitled. He was based near Colchester in Essex and when he realized that he was broke, decided that he should return to his camp and face the music. While waiting for his train at London's Liverpool Street Station, Fowler struck up an acquaintance with a Canadian officer,

Captain John J. Webber. Webber invited George Fowler back to his own camp, which also happened to be near Colchester. When the two men got to Cherry Tree Camp, they began sharing a bottle of whiskey. When the captain left the room though, he discovered on returning that his new friend had slipped off, taking with him not only the bottle of whiskey but also the officer's coat containing a Rolex watch and £5 in cash.

So far, George Fowler was guilty of nothing other than being absent without leave and stealing some money and a wristwatch, but instead of returning to Birch Camp, five miles from Colchester, he chose instead to stop first at a public house called the White Horse. There he met another black soldier, Private John Leatherberry, and since he now had some money, Fowler agreed to return to London with Leatherberry. It could not have been a very close association, because a few days later, Leatherberry could not even remember Fowler's name. At any event, the two men took a train to London and then spent two nights there. They returned to Colchester on Tuesday, 7 December, having spent the £5 which Fowler had stolen from the Canadian officer, and ended up being without money. When they reached Colchester, the two men visited a pub and then after it closed that night hired a taxi to take them back to their base at Birch. The following evening, the taxi was found abandoned in a lane near Birch, with no sign of the driver, a disabled man called Harry Hailstone.

Enquiries by the police showed that Harry Hailstone, after picking up two black soldiers from a pub, had stopped at his lodgings where he told his landlady that he had been engaged to drive two 'coloured soldiers' to Birch. When his corpse was found in a ditch two days later, the missing person enquiry at once turned into a murder hunt, for it was clear that the dead man had been beaten up and strangled. Blood had already been found on the seats of the taxi and the discovery of the owner's corpse came as little or no surprise.

There can seldom have been a more careless killer than George Fowler; the trail of clues which led to him was a clear as could be. The coat which he had stolen from Captain Webber was found in a ditch near the taxi and it bore bloodstains. The owner's name was marked inside and so the police were soon interviewing the Canadian officer, who at first was treated with some suspicion. However, somebody at Cherry Tree Camp remembered the black soldier who came back from London with the captain and revealed that the man had left his gasmask behind when he fled with Captain Webber's coat. This led at once to George Fowler, who could presumably feel the noose already tightening around his neck. He did what many another man in his position has done. At first, he lied his head off, but seeing that this was no use he struck a deal whereby in exchange for his own life, he would set the investigators on the track of the man Fowler claimed had actually committed the murder. This was, at least according to Fowler, John Leatherberry.

George Fowler made several statements, each more damning than the one before. In his final statement, he said that Leatherberry had suggested that they call a taxi to get back to the base and then rob the driver. He had also asked Fowler to let him wear his coat, because he was cold. This was of course the coat which Fowler had stolen a few days earlier from the Canadian officer. Fowler, by his own account, thought that the suggestion about robbing a taxi driver was a joke. When Fowler asked the taxi to stop, so that he might relieve himself, John Leatherberry unexpectedly set upon the driver and strangled him, while at the same time punching him repeatedly in the face and causing his nose to bleed. In this version of events, Fowler was no more than a hapless and quite innocent bystander. He had reluctantly helped Leatherberry to carry the body to a nearby ditch to hide it.

After Leatherberry was arrested and questioned, those investigating the murder knew that unless they were very careful, then one of the men present during the murder would escape justice entirely. John Leatherberry confirmed some of what Fowler had said, although he did not at first know whom they were talking about; he had not bothered to remember the name of the man with whom he spent a couple of days. He also had an alibi for the time of the murder; he was in bed with an

English girl. His alibi changed during the course of the questioning, but what was certain was that he was able to name at least one woman who would swear that he had been in London on the night that Harry Hailstone had been murdered. Leatherberry's account was that he had spent the evening of 6 December at the cinema with a girl in London and had also been seen at a place called the West India Club. Kaye Peters, the manageress of a café near the West India Club, testified that he had been in her café on 7 December and 8 December. In short, he had been nowhere near Colchester on the night that Harry Hailstone had been killed. He also had a woman, whose husband was a soldier serving abroad, who would testify that he had spent the night of 7 December with her at her home in East London.

Fortunately for the police, they had two very strong pieces of evidence which overturned the alibi which was presented to the court when the courts martial took place of Fowler and Leatherberry. The first part of this evidence consisted of the statements made by George Fowler. He was ready to admit having been present at the taxi driver's murder and to identify Leatherberry as having been the man who had actually killed Harry Hailstone. There was something even better though, which was forensic evidence which the prosecution at Leatherberry's court martial described as a quirk of fate which was 'almost fictional'.

There was no DNA testing in those days, but the presence of various blood types could be strongly indicative of guilt. Harry Hailstone's blood group was AB, which is shared by just two per cent of the population. Blood of this same type was found not only splashed on the coat which Leatherberry had been wearing, but traces of the same group were found under his fingernails. He claimed to have been in a fight in London, but even the most ferocious fight is unlikely to leave blood under the fingernails. However, if he had been dragging to a ditch the body of a man whose face was covered in blood from the beating he had received, then it would be quite feasible to expect blood to get all over the place.

Although there is probably no doubt that Fowler and Leatherberry were both guilty of the murder of the taxi driver, it remains the case that Leatherberry had a strong alibi and it was Fowler's evidence which convicted him. We will never know the extent of each man's culpability in the death of Harry Hailstone, but as is usual in such cases, there was most likely little to choose between them. This makes it rather unfair that Fowler, who was caught first and was so obviously guilty from the start, should have been able to strike a deal which brought his companion in crime to the scaffold. For when the two men were brought to trial at Ipswich in January 1944, they were tried separately, in different rooms of the same building. Fowler was convicted of murder, robbery and larceny, one of the charges relating to his theft of Captain Webber's coat, and he was then produced as the star prosecution witness at John Leatherberry's court martial. His evidence was compelling and Leatherberry was convicted and sentenced to death.

So it was that after the two courts martial, George Fowler was shipped back to the United States to begin serving his sentence of life imprisonment with hard labour, while John Leatherberry was sent to Shepton Mallet Prison to await execution. The process of review and confirmation of the sentence took several months to complete and on 16 May 1944 Tom Pierrepoint, assisted by his nephew Albert, hanged Leatherberry.

The next case at which we shall look is remarkable for the number of people who appealed for clemency for the condemned man, despite his having committed a brutal murder in the course of which he stabbed a man no fewer than sixteen times. It was perhaps the character of the victim which excited sympathy for the man convicted of his killing rather than anything else.

In 1944 Private Wiley Harris Jr was stationed in Northern Ireland with the 626th Ordnance Ammunition Company. His unit was stationed at Dromantine House, Poyntzpass in County Down. On 6 March 1944 Harris was given a 24-hour pass so that he could visit Belfast, the largest city in the province. Like any ordinary soldier, Wiley Harris headed for a bar and settled down there for a few drinks. He began at the American Red Cross Club in James Street, a place for black army personnel, before moving on to the Diamond Bar, where he met another member of his unit, Sergeant John W. London. At one point, Sergeant London had a whispered conversation with a man and then left the bar. He returned a short while later and confided in Wiley Harris that he had just had a most satisfactory encounter with a prostitute, which had been arranged with the man to whom he had spoken so furtively. When this same man, Harry Coogan, asked Harris if he wanted a woman, the young black soldier agreed immediately and a price of £1 was agreed. Coogan then pointed out a girl called Eileen Megaw, who was also in the bar, and suggested that the three of them go somewhere a little more convenient. This turned out to be a public air raid shelter in nearby Earl Street, which was empty. Harris handed over the pound to Eileen Megaw and Harry Coogan offered to stand guard outside and alert the couple if he saw any police officers approaching.

Once inside the shelter, Wiley Harris laid his coat on the floor but, in his own words;

> Before I could do what I intended to do Coogan shouted the Police were coming. On going outside I could see no one about so I asked the girl to go to the shelter with me. She said no, so I asked for my money back

This of course is an ancient trick, often worked by a husband-and-wife team, to cheat men of their money. Had he been a little more worldly-wise, then Wiley Harris would probably not have fallen so readily for it. Sometimes such affairs end peacefully, at other times they descend into violence, which was what happened on this occasion.

Harris' statement continued, 'I asked the girl for my money. The man said, "She can't give you the money"'. At this point things became very lively and there were a number of witnesses, because it was the sort of area where a crowd soon began to gather if it looked as though a fight might be about to develop. Harris said, 'The girl started to run and I grabbed her'.

The young woman made a break for it, dropping the pound's worth of coins as she did so. When Harris bent down to retrieve his money, Harry Coogan shouted to the gathering onlookers, 'This nigger is going to stab this woman but I'll not let him!' He then lashed out at Harris, catching him in the face. A woman called Bridget Murdoch grabbed Coogan's arm at this point and tried to restrain him, telling him not to hit the soldier. Harris might have been gullible enough to fall for such an old swindle in the first place, but he was no coward. When he realized that Harry Coogan meant not only to cheat him of his money but also to beat him up, he immediately pulled out a knife and plunged it into the pimp, withdrawing it and then thrusting it in and out fifteen times more.

Neighbours came out to see what the disturbance was all about. Annie Murdoch, who lived at 158 Earl Street, was sitting at home listening to the radio. Her sister-in-law Bridget called for her to come and see the fight. She witnessed Harry Coogan call Harris a nigger and then strike him in the face. She then saw Wiley Harris leap at the other man and stab him repeatedly. The police were called, but by the time Head Constable Armstrong and Sergeant Herron got to the scene, Coogan was dead and there was no sign of his assailant.

After stabbing Coogan, Harris returned to the American Red Cross Club, where he was seen washing blood from his uniform. Sergeant London and Private Fils both saw him doing so and made statements accordingly. Private Fils knew Harris, for he had been drinking with him in the Diamond Bar before the other man had gone off with Coogan and the young woman. Sergeant London too knew a fair bit about the situation, for he had already had sex that evening with Eileen Megaw.

It did not take very long for the civilian police to work out that an American serviceman had been responsible for the stabbing and, following Wiley Harris' arrest on the same day that he had stabbed Harry Coogan to death, things moved very quickly. His court martial, in Belfast's Victoria Barracks, took place just 11 days later. The evidence was plain enough, that he had stabbed Coogan to death, but Harris pleaded that this had been self-defence, which would have reduced the offence to manslaughter if accepted by the court. It was not. It was probably the evidence of Dr James Crilly, the man who had examined Coogan's body at the Mater Hospital in Belfast, which caused the court to look unfavourably on returning such a verdict. Dr Crilly told the court that he had identified a total of sixteen separate wounds to Coogan's body. A man who feels threatened might perhaps lash out desperately with a weapon. To hack away in such a relentless way though suggested something a good deal more savage than merely a man defending himself against a fairly low-key assault.

Private Harris was found guilty of murder and sentenced to death, whereupon something quite extraordinary happened. Whether it was because a lot of people in Belfast, as in the rest of the United Kingdom, had observed with distaste the segregation of the American army, or possibly because of the sordid behaviour of the victim in the case, who was at best a pimp and a swindler, a campaign began to save Wiley Harris' life. Not only were petitions organized in Northern Ireland, but the main churches united in opposing the execution of the soldier whom they apparently believed had received a raw deal. Among those who spoke out publicly in favour of a reprieve for Wiley Harris were the Lord Mayor of Belfast, the Lord Bishop of Down, the Moderator of the General Assembly and various other churchmen from the Methodists to the Presbyterians and the Catholic Church. In a city noted for its religious divisions, there was an astonishing unanimity on this matter. Even more surprising was the fact that the Leader of the House of Lords in London, Viscount Cranborne, sent a telegram to President Roosevelt claiming that 99 per cent of people in Britain opposed the execution of Wiley Harris and that it would damage Anglo-American relations should he be hanged.

It was all to no avail. On the morning of 26 May 1944, Private Wiley Harris Jr was hanged at Shepton Mallet Prison.

Chapter 11

The Murder of Sir Eric Teichman

All the murders at which we have so far looked have been of ordinary and unremarkable individuals; taxi drivers, unfaithful lovers and soldiers who fell foul of men with uncontrollable tempers or sudden homicidal urges. But one of the murders committed by American soldiers between 1942 and 1945 was in a different category entirely. The victim was a man of some consequence and his death was a major item of news at the time, which even displaced news about the war in Europe and the Far East. To understand the significance of this particular murder, that of Sir Eric Teichman, we must begin by explaining who he was and why his death should have caused more shock than that of any of the other murders explored in this book.

Eric Teichman came from a fairly well-to-do family and as a young man entered the British consular service. He was of a particular type which was recognizable during the days when the British Empire was still a powerful force in world affairs. Although he was nominally a diplomat, Teichman was also a secret agent. His chief area of interest was China and he held various official posts there, but also undertook 'special missions' and 'fact-finding expeditions'. Acknowledged as an expert in the field of Oriental studies, Teichman had written a number of books which had to been published to critical acclaim. Among these were *Travels of a Consular Officer in Eastern Tibet: Together with a History of the Relations Between China, Tibet and India*, 1922, *Journey to Turkistan*, 1937 and *Affairs of China: A Survey of the Recent History and Present Circumstances of the Republic of China*, 1938. Although he had theoretically retired in 1936, Teichman was recalled to government service in 1942 and became advisor to the British Embassy at Chunking, in China. After various adventures there, he returned to England in 1944 and just a few days after coming home, was murdered.

Home for Sir Eric Teichman was an enormous mansion in Norfolk, called Honingham Hall. This was built in the early seventeenth century, although it has now been demolished. It was surrounded by a great deal of land, 3,000 acres, and had been bought in 1935 by Teichman, who intended that he and his wife should retire there when he had finished travelling around the Far East on behalf of the government. During the Second World War, Sir Eric Teichman allowed a large part of the hall to be taken over by Barnardo's and used as a children's home.

On the afternoon of Sunday, 3 December 1944, Teichman was sitting at home with his wife, relaxing after lunch. From somewhere on the estate came the sound of shooting. Not just one or two shots, but a perfect fusillade of firing. He may have been 60 years old, retired and disabled, but Eric Teichman's life had been more dangerous and exciting than most people's and when he heard the sound of gunfire on his property, he at once left the house to investigate. There had been trouble with poachers before and Teichman was determined to confront whoever was shooting without permission on his estate. Due to a riding accident 10 years before, in which he had broken his spine, Teichman was unable to stand fully upright and so walked doubled over in a peculiar fashion. As he left the house at two o'clock that Sunday afternoon, nobody could know that this would be the last time anybody other than his killer would ever set eyes upon him again while he was still alive.

When Sir Eric Teichman left his home that December afternoon, he was about to come into contact with a somebody whose character and experiences were very different to his own. Private George Smith was 28 years of age and had been in the army for two years. He was an American soldier and cook at a nearby airfield. During the course of the time he been in the army, he had somehow managed to be court-martialled no fewer than eight times! This averages out at a court martial every three months. Smith, as was later established by the psychiatrists who examined him, was a man with very little self-control and a low threshold for anger. In short, it took very little to cause him to lose his temper and react with violence. All this was bad enough, but he had, on that Sunday, been drinking heavily. By his own reckoning, he had consumed around fifteen cups of beer. The combination of a hair-trigger temper and the lowering of inhibitions brought on by intoxication were to prove quite literally lethal that day.

George Smith had it in mind to go hunting and persuaded another man who had been part of the group who were drinking that day to go with him. Private Leonard S. Wojtacha was not quite such a rebel and malcontent as Smith and probably only went along with him that day as a bit of fun. The two men took M1 carbines from the armoury, along with a box of ammunition, and left the airfield where they were stationed in search of what might just have been a bit of high-spirited fun. According to Wojtacha, George Smith began by shooting a cow in the leg and then began firing at oil drums and other inanimate objects. They entered the grounds of Honingham Hall, where the two of them took pot-shots, firstly at blackbirds and then a squirrel which they had spotted scampering from branch to branch. It was at this point that Wojtacha saw an old man approaching and warned his companion that they were no longer alone.

Sir Eric Teichman demanded to know the names of the two men he had found trespassing, whereupon George Smith said, 'Get back pop!' and fired a single shot, which struck Teichman in the right cheek, from where it was deflected downwards, shattering the jaw and ploughing through various internal organs in the chest before exiting from his left shoulder blade. The wounded man fell to the ground, where he died almost immediately. The reaction of the two Americans to this incident is telling. Neither made any attempt to ascertain if the man was dead or merely injured. They both bolted and their only concern was to try and clean the barrels of their rifles in order to disguise the fact that their weapons had recently been fired.

When Teichman did not come back after going to confront the supposed poachers, his wife became uneasy and contacted the police. By this time, it was getting dark and a perfunctory search found nothing. Some personnel at the local American base offered their assistance, but they too did not come across anything. To the police, this was hardly a serious matter. Men walk out of their houses all the time. Sometimes, there has been an argument with their wives, at others they have just chosen to visit a public house. After seeing nothing to cause them alarm, they left and assured Lady Ellen that her husband would probably come home before too long.

The afternoon turned to evening without any sign of Eric Teichman's return. Whatever the police might say, based on their experiences with missing persons, Teichman's wife knew very well that something was amiss. There was no question of sleeping and a little after midnight, Lady Ellen enlisted the help of her chauffeur and a district nurse called Victoria Childerhouse. It was the nurse who, at about one o'clock in the morning, stumbled over the corpse of Eric Teichman. It was obvious that he was dead and had been for some time, because the body was stone cold.

At first light that day, the police returned to Honingham Hall and Inspector Garner arrived with a photographer and officers who would comb the scene for clues. One thing was found almost immediately. The bullet which had killed Eric Teichman had expended most of its energy in smashing through flesh and bone. When it exited the left shoulder, it merely popped out and travelled another few feet before dropping to the ground. As soon as the copper-jacketed bullet was found, it was obvious that this was no ordinary case of poaching which had resulted perhaps in a tragic accident. This was a military bullet, fired either from an American carbine or a British Lee-Enfield rifle. Poachers were far more likely to have been using a shotgun. At once, the police knew that the focus for their enquiries would have to be one of the army bases in that part of Norfolk. By Tuesday, the day that the inquest was to begin, the field had been narrowed even further. Something else was obvious and that was this was almost certainly no accidental death, a stray bullet fired from a long way away which had the misfortune to strike somebody out of sight of the shooter. The amount of damage which the bullet had wrought to the elderly man's body, tearing through sinew and bone, driving through the upper torso and still having sufficient energy left to leave the body and fly another few feet, showed that it must have been fired at close range, certainly no more than a few yards.

On Tuesday morning the Assistant Chief Constable for Norfolk told reporters;

> Sir Eric Teichman was definitely shot by a rifle bullet. A shot has been found but we have not yet had it tested. I think that it is a .300 but I cannot definitely say yet that it came from a Service rifle. There have been a lot of complaints of poaching.

The reference to poaching was probably designed as a red herring, so that the owner of the rifle which had fired the bullet that killed Teichman would not be panicked into trying to dispose of it. At any rate, by the end of the day the police, working in cooperation with the American military, were checking every M1 rifle at the nearby bases. It did not take long to match the bullet with the carbine which had fired it. The murder took place on Sunday and then on Thursday, 7 December, it was announced by the American authorities that George Smith had been charged with the murder and Leonard Wojtacha as an accessory.

Those investigating had spent the day after Sir Eric's death examining all the rifles at the American base and seeing if any of them could be matched to the bullet which had been recovered. On 5 December, while this process was still being conducted, George Smith came up to the table in the mess hall where Wojtacha was eating with some friends and said, according to witnesses, 'Don't say anything. Let them find out for themselves.'

The following day, the military police interviewed Leonard Wojtacha and he at once made a statement which incriminated Smith. It had not taken Wojtacha long to realize the peril in which he now found himself; in hazard of his very life. When two people set out to commit a crime and one of them kills somebody in the commission of the crime, then both are held to be equally guilty in the eyes of the law. The concept of 'common purpose' comes into play. Under this doctrine, Leonard Wojtacha was considered every bit as guilty of murder as the man who actually pulled the trigger. He had accordingly thought it better to confess his involvement in the trespassing in the grounds of Honingham Hall and exculpate himself from blame by explaining how the whole idea had been Smith's and that it was Smith who had shot Sir Eric.

As a reward for his cooperation and readiness to point the finger at the one who had actually fired at the unarmed man, the charge against Leonard Wojtacha was not murder, but being an accessory to murder. This left George Smith to face the consequences of his actions. Although he later retracted his statement, Smith, when questioned, at once admitted shooting the owner of Honingham Hall. When he was first interviewed by the Provost Marshal, he said;

> Some of us had been drinking beer. I drank about fifteen coffee cups of beer. We went up in the woods. I saw a squirrel and fired one clip of 15 shots. One of us said 'There's an old man.' I think I saw him first and made the remark. I don't remember the old man saying anything to me nor do I remember saying anything to him. I raised my gun to my side, pointed it at the old man and fired one shot. I saw the old man fall.

There can seldom have been a more dispassionate and cold-blooded confession to murder.

Defending such an unattractive individual, and of course self-confessed murderer, was going to prove no easy task for the officers assigned to George Smith's defence. His alleged statement was not the only evidence against him by the time that the court martial began on Monday, 8 January 1945 at Attlebridge Air Base. There was the fact that the bullet which had killed Teichman had been matched to George Smith's rifle and also there was the awkward circumstance that the prosecution had an eyewitness to the murder, Smith's one-time hunting partner.

The trial was held in the room which was used during the week as a gymnasium and on Sundays as a chapel. So great was the interest in the case of the man accused of murdering Sir Eric Teichman that extra seating was installed, so that in total about 400 people were present in the court. There had been particular demand for places by British lawyers, keen to watch an American murder trial and see in what way, if any, it differed from the kind with which they were themselves familiar. Smith was flanked by his defence counsel, Major Peter Deisch and First Lieutenant Sokarl. The only hope was to show that George Smith suffered from such an abnormality of mind that he was not really responsible for his actions. As part of this strategy, the court martial had to adjourn from time to time, so that Smith could attend hospital appointments. The whole aim was to portray him as a mentally-ill man whom it would be wrong to hang.

Much of the court martial was taken up with the undisputed facts of the murder and the prosecution agreed that once he had been arrested, Smith had cooperated fully with the police in revisiting the scene of the crime and helping them to reconstruct what had happened that day. The defence did not object to details of his eight previous courts martial being introduced as evidence, because it all helped in the picture which they were attempting to paint of a man who simply could not control himself. The medical evidence as to George Smith's state of mind was inconclusive. Major L. Alexander was a specialist in neurology and psychiatry, attached to a US Army hospital in England. He said, among other things, that Smith displayed 'a constitutional psychopathic condition, emotional instability, and an explosive, primitive, sadistic aggressiveness'. He went on to give it as his opinion that 'His mental deficiency was borderline, and his mental age was about nine years'. Major Alexander ended his report by indicating that the murder which George Smith committed was, for him, an automatic impulse. He was, in short, saying that Smith had learning difficulties, combined with a fierce and uncontrollable temper.

The fact that Smith had a mental age of just nine was not as significant as might at first be thought. In answer to questions, Major Alexander revealed that during the First World War, the average mental age of American soldiers was just 12. During the Second World War, it had risen to 13 or 14. In other words, an awful lot of the conscripted men in the army had fairly low IQs and were mentally more like adolescents than adult men.

The details which emerged of George Smith's early life were depressing and certainly suggested a man who was far from normal. He recalled how as a child he had had two pet mice. He cut off their tails, because he thought it would be funny to have mice with bobtails. This kind of casual cruelty to animals in childhood is often the mark of worse things to come as an adult. It is, together with fire-raising, one of the signs of psychopathy.

Another professional who had been given the opportunity to examine George Smith was Dr John Vincent Morris, of the Little Plumstead Hall Institution, Norwich. He too was an expert on mental illness and developmental delays. He gave it as his opinion that George Smith was an anti-social type who deliberately refused to conform to any rules or codes of conduct, which accounted for the fact that he was regularly facing courts martial, this being the ninth. Dr Morris said that the accused man had talked about the shooting with as much emotion as a man who talked of killing a rabbit. He suspected that Smith had carried out the murder because, 'Sir Eric interfered with his pleasure, and he acted under an uncontrollable impulse'.

By the time that George Smith was being tried for his life, the charge against Leonard Wojtacha had been reduced to one of negligently discharging his weapon. It was obvious that he had had no part in the death of Sir Eric Teichman and had not the faintest notion that Smith was going to commit murder that afternoon. During his evidence, Wojtacha told how George Smith had shot a cow in the leg and then started laughing uncontrollably when the beast began making distressed noises and running around with the injured leg in the air. He further related that when they had returned to base after the shooting of Sir Eric, he had been frightened, but Smith had seemed quite unaffected by what he had done.

The only question which really had to be determined, if George Smith was to escape the gallows, was a simple one; did he know what killing a man as he had done that December afternoon was wrong? Despite all the talk of his disturbed childhood, there was ultimately little suggestion that he did not understand the difference between right and wrong. He simply chose to pursue his own course, regardless of what society thought was proper behaviour. The relevant part of the court's judgement read as follows;

> In effect, the two Army psychiatrists agreed that accused knew right from wrong, and that he was sane. The civilian psychiatrist testified that accused might at times be able to distinguish right from wrong, but that he could not adhere to the right and in this instance acted upon the uncontrollable impulse of a diseased brain. The Army psychiatrists were of the contrary opinion and testified that accused had the ability, though somewhat impaired, to adhere to the right, and that his actions here involved were not quite automatic.

In the end, the members of the court martial took what was perhaps the common-sense approach and decided that George Smith was more bad than mad. On 12 January 1945, he was found guilty of murder and sentenced to death by hanging.

At one o'clock in the morning of 8 May 1945, coincidentally the very day that the German army surrendered unconditionally to the Allies, George Smith was led to the gallows and hanged by Tom Pierrepoint, assisted by Herbert Morris.

Chapter 12

On the Nature of Firing Squads

The use of firing squads as a means of execution has almost invariably had military connotations. This is perhaps because soldiers usually have rifles near at hand and it is easy enough to arrange for a group of them to aim their weapons at somebody. This is, after all, the whole practical purpose of armies in the field! The concept underlying the firing squad, though, pre-dates the invention of guns by thousands of years.

The earliest books of the Bible, dating back perhaps three or four thousand years, set out the penalty of stoning to death. This was a way of ensuring that the whole community took part in inflicting death upon anybody who transgressed in certain specified ways against the rules of the Bronze Age society of ancient Israel. This meant that not only would the responsibility for the victim's death be distributed among the whole community, rather than falling only upon one person acting as executioner, but also that society generally could express their united condemnation of whatever act the condemned man or woman had been culpable. This old tradition is still practised in one or two Muslim countries to this very day. From hurling stones, it was a natural progression to firing arrows instead and from the entire community joining in, it made more sense to choose a few people to represent everybody else. This was something which happened in parts of Europe at the time of the Roman Empire. In Britain, King Edmund the Martyr was killed in this way by Vikings, around 870 AD. He was simply tied to a tree and arrows were fired at him until he was dead. Some readers may also be familiar with medieval paintings of the death of St Sebastian, which took place under similar circumstances in 288 AD. This was a very popular subject for artists in the sixteenth and seventeenth centuries.

The first firing squads using guns were recorded during the English Civil War. In 1648, for example, after the city of Colchester was taken by the Parliamentarians, it was decided to punish those who had held out against the siege by shooting their leaders. Sir George Lisle and Sir Charles Lucas were executed near the castle and later became known as the 'Royalist Martyrs'. By the eighteenth century, Britain had perfected both the method of using firing squads and also the circumstances under which they might be used. Shooting was seen as an honourable death, much preferable to hanging, and was used exclusively by the armed forces, either for punishing one of their own or, from time to time, for disposing of spies. When shooting a British soldier, the convention arose that those making up the firing party should be chosen from the condemned man's own unit. In this way, the execution could be viewed as a team effort and when a deserter or mutineer was shot, it showed that even his fellow soldiers disapproved of and rejected the victim's conduct.

The British method of execution by firing squad was exported to the colonies, in particular America. There too 'honourable death by powder and shot', as it was quaintly known, was thought to be fitting to a gentleman in a way that be suspended from the gallows was not. In 1780, during the American War of Independence, the head of the British Secret Service in America was Major John Andre. Following the treachery of Benedict Arnold, who tried to betray his own side by surrendering the West Point Academy to the British, Major Andre was captured in civilian clothes and tried as a spy.

Although he defended himself skilfully against the charge of espionage, there was little doubt as to what verdict the court which tried him would deliver. He was duly convicted and sentenced to death. Although not afraid to die, Andre was appalled that he was to hang and petitioned the American authorities to allow him what he described as a 'gentleman's' death, that is to say being shot by a firing squad. He could not endure the idea of hanging from a gibbet, although that was indeed to be his fate. Major Andre's attitude shows that by the end of the eighteenth century, the idea was firmly fixed in the minds of many, on both sides of the Atlantic, that being executed by firing squad was the most acceptable way to suffer execution.

Firing squads were not at all uncommon during the American Civil War and both sides used them pretty freely as a means of making a public display to discourage those thinking of deserting. On 5 September 1863, ten deserters from the 3rd North Carolina Infantry were shot simultaneously. The 10 September edition of the *Richmond Daily Dispatch* described in detail what happened. Ten stakes had been set up and the prisoners were marched to their deaths by the regimental band playing the Dead March. The newspaper reported that, 'The bearing of the prisoners was calm and self-possessed, and they marched to the place of their execution with a step as accurate in its cadence as that of the guard who conducted them.' All of the men met their deaths bravely.

This might be a good time to pause and think about the kind of death inflicted by firing squads. There is a popular belief that being shot through the heart by half a dozen bullets must be a fairly swift way to die. After all, if the heart is torn to pieces, one must lose consciousness almost immediately and feel nothing further, or so the reasoning goes. It is not so. In fact, execution by firing squad is apt to be a protracted and painful business for the victim. We know this without a shadow of a doubt as a result of an extraordinary experiment carried out in the United States in 1938.

The first thing to bear in mind is that firing with a heavy military rifle from a standing position, rather than laying on the ground or kneeling, is likely to be a chancy affair as far as hitting the target accurately is concerned. In warfare, this seldom matters. As long as your troops are sending a hail of bullets in the general direction of the enemy; that is all that matters. When they are trying to hit a small piece of white material pinned to the chest of a man standing 20 yards away though, it can be a different matter entirely. Most readers will have heard of Eddie Slovik, the last person to executed by the US Army for desertion. When Slovik was shot on 31 January 1945, the firing party consisted of twelve men, eleven of whose rifles were loaded with live ammunition. Only four of the bullets hit the heart. Others struck Slovik's arm, shoulder and neck, while others hit various parts of his torso. This was at very close range, but he did not die at once. The order was given to reload the rifles, but fortunately, by the time this was done, Eddie Slovik was dead.

How long does it take a man to die after being executed by a firing squad, one which manages to deliver most of its bullets to the heart? We know precisely and the answer is not a pleasant one. A few states in America have used firing squads as their official means of capital punishment. In one of these, Utah, a condemned man agreed to cooperate with doctors to see just what happens when somebody is executed in this way. John Deering was an unremarkable murderer who was sentenced to death for killing a man in Salt Lake City. On 31 October 1938, he faced a firing squad at the Sugar House Penitentiary, on the outskirts of Salt Lake City. The prison doctor, Stephen H. Besley, asked Deering if he would help in some research which the doctor was conducting. Specifically, he wanted to connect an electrocardiogram to the condemned man's wrists so that he could record how being shot affected the working of the heart. It was a peculiar investigation, but John Deering agreed to take part.

John Deering must have had a very lively and somewhat dark sense of humour. He was born in 1898 and executed in 1938. Shortly before his execution, he said, 'I'm going out there and prove that those guys who said life begins at 40 are cockeyed liars.' The readings from Dr Besley's electrocardiogram are fascinating. While Deering was being prepared for execution by having a target pinned to his shirt, his heart was beating at a normal 72 beats a minute. Once he was strapped to the chair where he would die though, his heart rate had soared to an almost incredible 180 beats a minute. When the five marksmen, one firing a blank round, opened fire, four bullets smashed into Deering's chest. His heart spasmed and convulsed for a few seconds, before stopping beating altogether after 15 seconds. John Deering did not die though.

For over a minute, he continued breathing and struggling against his bonds. It took him over two minutes to die, presumably in agony. This is not all the way we imagine things should be when a man has been shot through the heart.

A word needs to be said about the customary practice, of which most readers will have heard, of including a blank round in the rifle of one man making up a firing squad. This has happened in all British and American executions of this kind in the twentieth century. The idea of having a blank, sometimes known as a 'conscience round', is that every one of the men making up the firing party will be able to believe that perhaps he was not responsible for the death of a fellow being. It is of course, all nonsense. Anybody who has ever fired a military rifle will know the sharp kick of the recoil which strike the shoulder when the trigger is pulled. This is the reaction to the heavy bullet leaving the barrel of the gun. As we know from our childhood physics lessons, for every action there is an equal and opposite reaction. This means that as the bullet moves forward from the muzzle with great energy, a similar and equal amount of energy must be projected backwards, into the shoulder of the person firing the weapon. The 'kick' from a rifle can be a fearsome thing and quite capable of leaving an inexperienced shooter's shoulder bruised. This is not of course experienced when a blank round is fired. In that case only a puff of hot gas and burnt powdery residue leaves the gun. There is little recoil under such circumstances.

In 1915, a British soldier serving in France during the First World War was selected to be part of a firing squad, along with eleven other men, to execute a deserter. The men were handed rifles which had all been jumbled up together. The reason for this was that eleven of the weapons had been loaded with live .303 rounds and one contained a blank. W.A. Quinton wrote after the war that, 'I had the satisfaction of knowing that as soon as I fired, from the absence of any recoil that I had merely fired a blank cartridge'. In the most recent execution by firing squad in the United States, that of Ronnie Lee Gardner in Utah in 2010, an attempt was made to get around this problem. Of the five weapons used, four had ordinary bullets and one had a live round in which the metal-jacketed bullet had been removed and replaced by one made of wax. Whether a light projectile made of wax would give the same recoil as a standard round is open to question.

When the Second World War began, the US Army had rather got out of the habit of shooting people by the use of firing squads. The British and French used firing squads extensively during the First World War, the British for desertion and the French mainly for mutiny. The Americans though only executed their troops during that war for murder and rape. The eleven executions carried out following courts martial were by hanging, rather than shooting. It was generally assumed that the same would be true of the Second World War when the United States entered that conflict in partnership with Britain. It was of course for this reason that the Americans built a new execution block at Shepton Mallet Prison when they moved in; they expected to hang any soldiers condemned to death, rather than shooting them. Nevertheless, two men were executed by firing squad at Shepton Mallet and a certain amount of mystery attached itself to this.

Two explanations have been advanced for the use of firing squads to deal with Alex Miranda and Benjamin Pyegate, shot within six months of each other in 1944. The first of these supposed explanations is that they murdered fellow soldiers and the second is that the crimes were actually committed on military bases. Either or both of these circumstances are said to have been sufficient to alter the cases of the two men and entitle them to executions by shooting, instead of hanging. Both reasons fail, because as we saw in Chapter 6, David Cobb also killed a soldier on a military base and he was hanged. Could it be that race played a role in the decision to hang Cobb for exactly the same type of offence for which Miranda and Pyegate were accorded the more respectable death of facing a firing squad? This is unlikely, because Miranda was Hispanic and Benjamin Pyegate was black. There is currently no convincing explanation as to why these men were singled out for a different form of execution.

Let us look at the circumstances surrounding the first execution by 'musketry', as the quaint wording of the sentence passed put it, carried out by the US Army in the twentieth century. We have already looked at the origin of this practice and the executions which the Americans organized were no different from anybody else's. The crimes which led up to them though are of some interest.

In 1944, the 42nd Field Artillery Battalion, a unit of the US Army, was stationed at Broomhill Camp, on the outskirts of the Devon town of Honiton. On the evening of 4 March 1944, 20-year-old Private Alex Miranda went into Honiton for a drinking spree. The exact degree of his intoxication was the subject of intense debate, because his defence to the subsequent charge of murder which he faced was founded entirely upon the assertion that he was so drunk that he did not know what he was doing. In other words, at his trial he claimed that he was so inebriated that he was not responsible for his actions.

After spending that Saturday evening drinking, Miranda happened to clash with the local civilian police in what was an exceedingly trivial incident, but one which apparently triggered a murder later that night. At 12:15 am on the morning of Sunday 5 March, Sergeant William Durbin and Police Constable North came across Alex Miranda urinating in the doorway of a shop on Honiton High Street. They remonstrated with him and advised him that this kind of behaviour was not acceptable, whereupon Miranda became, in the words of the police officers, 'nasty and abusive'. Among other things, he described Durbin as a 'fine, fat sergeant', which did not go down too well. As a result of this, they arrested Miranda and took him to the police station, where he threatened to 'rip out their guts'. They rang the American base, who send a Military Policeman to collect the drunken soldier.

One thing which the police noticed, and was regarded as perhaps significant in the light of what subsequently happened, was that Miranda displayed a marked antipathy towards sergeants. It was not limited to calling Sergeant Durbin a 'fine, fat sergeant'. Some officers left the station to go to help a couple of sergeants who had been in an accident. When he overheard this being discussed, Miranda remarked loudly, 'I hope they rip their guts out!' As Sergeant Durbin later said in his statement, Miranda 'seemed to have sergeants in mind'.

So far, this could hardly be a more trifling and insignificant business. The MPs who collected Miranda from Honiton Police Station didn't take the matter seriously. Back at the base, they held him in the guardhouse for a quarter of an hour and then told him to go to his own hut and sleep it off. As far as they were concerned, it was all over and done with and had Private Miranda just have gone to bed at that point, then nothing further would have happened. He didn't go to bed though. He arrived at the hut where he was staying in a very angry mood and looking for trouble. According to the evidence given at the court martial, he was 'noisy and boisterous' when he entered the hut. It was now about 1:00 am and everybody else was sleeping; at least they were, until Miranda woke some of them by his behaviour.

There is still no reason at all why things could not simply have proceeded to their logical conclusion, that is to say the drunk man stumbling to his bed and then waking up next morning with a hangover and facing some chaffing from those with whom he shared the hut. It seems though that Miranda was obsessed with what Sergeant Thomas Evison, who was also sleeping in the hut, might say to him the next day. Evison was a strict disciplinarian and to one of the men whom he had awoken, Alex Miranda expressed the fear that Evison would 'ride' him about the fact that he had been brought back to base after falling foul of the local police. Thomas Evison was snoring loudly and Miranda went over to the sleeping man and shook him hard, telling him to stop snoring. Evison woke up and, most reasonably, told Miranda to let him alone and to go to bed and do his own snoring. This response served only to infuriate Miranda. We have already seen that somebody had gained the impression that night that Alex Miranda, 'seemed to have sergeants in mind'. This would certainly go some way towards explaining why he did not seem able to leave Sergeant Evison alone to carry on sleeping peacefully.

After Sergeant Evison had gone back to sleep and was once again snoring, Miranda lit a cigarette and stood brooding. Another soldier asked him what was wrong and he said that he feared that Evison would punish him, when he found out that he had been picked up for urinating in the street. At last, he seemed to make up his mind about something, for he extinguished his cigarette and strode off to another part of the hut, the place where the weapons were stored in a rack. He returned with an M1 carbine and went straight over to where Thomas Evison lay snoring and fired a single shot at the sleeping man's forehead, killing him instantly. The shot woke everybody else and Private Alex Miranda soon found himself under arrest once more, this time for something infinitely more serious than urinating in a shop doorway. The rifle had been practically pressed against the sergeant's forehead and, according to Captain Singley, the Battalion Medical Officer, the bullet had entered the forehead, passed through the brain and exited from the back of the head, from where it had also passed through a wooden part of the bed and a carton of cigarettes, before becoming buried in the wall. Brain matter was exuded from the hole in Sergeant Evison's forehead and spinal fluid was leaking out of the exit wound. Little wonder then that he died within minutes of being shot.

As he was led off, witnesses said that Miranda was giggling hysterically and told them that their troubles were all over, because he had shot the hated sergeant. Their troubles might have been all over, but his were just beginning. He was charged with murder and from the very beginning, it was plain that the prosecution at his court martial were determined to demand the death penalty.

Alex F. Miranda was charged with violating the 92nd Article of War, which forbids murder and was duly brought before a court martial. His defence was a simple one. It was never in dispute that he had shot Sergeant Evison dead. It was claimed though that he had been so drunk at the time that he had been unable fully to appreciate the consequences of his actions. There were two problems with this defence. In the first place, if a person voluntarily becomes intoxicated, then he cannot afterwards claim that his actions were involuntary. In other words, if you choose to get drunk, then you must know beforehand that you might say or do things which you would not generally do and should take this into consideration before embarking upon becoming drunk. Drunkenness has never been any sort of defence for a charge of murder, either in Britain or the United States.

There was a second, and even more damning, reason that Miranda's defence to the charge of murder was unlikely to succeed. One can perhaps imagine a man who is so catastrophically drunk that he really does not know what he is doing, even if this does not provide an excuse in law. None of the witnesses who came into contact with Alex Miranda after he had been drinking on the night of 4 March formed the impression that he was in such a state. He was not incoherent through drink; on the contrary, he had various rational conversations, both with the civilian and military police, as well as soldiers in his hut. The fact that he went off to find a gun also told against him. This was not a case of a man snatching up the first thing which came to hand and using it as a weapon. All the indications were that Alex Miranda was in full command of himself in the early hours of 5 March 1944 and had committed a cold-blooded and deliberate crime.

Many years later, it was suggested that the court may have been racially prejudiced again the defendant in this case because he was Hispanic and that it was this which caused them to bring in a verdict of murder, rather than manslaughter, and also to impose the death penalty instead of sending Miranda to prison. In deciding what penalty Miranda should face after his conviction, a member of the court, Lieutenant-Colonel White E. Gibson, made derogatory comments about Hispanics, saying that they 'are undemonstrative and uncommunicative, as well as being inclined to violence when drinking', which hardly suggests the proper degree of judicial impartiality, to say the very least. It had not helped Alex Miranda's case that he had refused to give evidence and be cross-examined.

Perhaps more to the point was the suggestion made by one member of the court that Miranda would have to be executed as an example to others. Had he killed another private, then it is conceivable that imprisonment might have been imposed, rather than death. It was felt though that the fact that he had murdered an NCO meant that if good order was to be maintained, then he must be executed.

The sentence of the court martial was that Alex F. Miranda should 'suffer death by musketry'. As has already been remarked, it is not known why Miranda should have been singled out for this, instead of being hanged. At any rate, the procedure to be followed was set out in painstaking detail in a document entitled, 'Procedure for Military Executions'. This covered every conceivable aspect of arranging how to put a man to death by means of a firing squad. It makes chilling reading; 'Cause a post with proper rings placed therein for securing the prisoner in an upright position to be erected at the place of execution' . . . 'Provide straps to secure the prisoner to the post at waist and ankles' . . . 'Provide a black hood to cover the head of the prisoner'. Nothing is overlooked, up to and including the correct way to ensure that there should be some uncertainty in the mind of the soldiers making up the firing squad as to whether it was their shot which was responsible for a man's death. The officer in charge should, 'Cause eight rifles to be loaded in his presence. Not more than three nor less than one will be loaded with blank ammunition. He will place the rifles at random in the rack provided for that purpose.'

The execution was scheduled for the morning of 30 May 1944. Unlike hangings, which took place at 1:00 am, executions by firing squad traditionally took place at dawn, a custom followed by most nations, including Britain, during the First World War. In Britain, those witnessing executions were only the people who had to be there, the governor of the prison, doctor, chaplain and so on. There was certainly no provision for witnesses just for the sake of it. The American method was very different. Albert Pierrepoint wrote feelingly of the cramped conditions in the execution chamber at Shepton Mallet when he and his uncle hanged men there. It was just the same for executions by shooting. In addition to the officer and men who made up the firing squad, there were many others present whose role was simply to see that justice had been done.

It was to the witnesses that May morning that Major Cullen, who was in charge of the execution, addressed the following words;

> Gentlemen, let me have your attention please. As you know, the personnel here this morning are to carry out the sentence of a General Court Martial, to inflict death upon Private Alex F. Miranda, who was convicted of the violation of the 92nd Article of War, murder. This is the first time we have carried out the death penalty here by shooting. Our procedure is a little bit easier and we hope to carry it through in the proper manner. The witnesses will leave here, following my departure, and assigned to your proper places by Captain Boye. There will be nothing to do except to observe the proceedings. The medical personnel, after the volley has been fired, will be directed to make their examination. Now, this is not an occasion for any levity or joking of any sort, and I will like to say that I appreciate utmost silence by witnesses particularly during the proceedings. Those of you, who have not yet had your breakfast, may get it in the mess immediately following the execution. Are there any questions?

There were no questions and so the grisly process of putting a man to death was begun.

The execution took place against the wall in the prison yard which is shown in Illustration 16. It was not ideal, but since this was a purely private affair involving only Americans, it was not thought appropriate to shoot Miranda anywhere else other than within the prison itself. Sandbags were piled up behind the post to which the condemned prisoner was strapped, to prevent any bullets ricocheting around. Once he had been fixed in place, with a small white target pinned over his heart, the chaplain had a last few words with Miranda, who said, 'Pray for me and may God have a place for you in Paradise'. The orders were given and the bullets smashed through the soldier's chest, killing him more or less immediately.

After his death, Alex Miranda's corpse was at first sent to Brookwood Cemetery, which is 30 miles or so from London. An American military cemetery existed here for soldiers who had died fighting in the First World War and also for those now dying in the Second World War. A small and neglected plot was now set aside for those who had been executed at Shepton Mallet. Miranda was not to rest peacefully though, for he was destined to be exhumed not once, but twice.

In 1948, all those soldiers who had been buried at Brookwood during the Second World War were transferred to a new American military cemetery near Cambridge, on land which had been donated by the university. Nobody wanted the men from Shepton Mallet to be interred with all the soldiers who had given their life for their country though. Like all those hanged or shot at Shepton Mallet, Alex Miranda had been dishonourably discharged from the army before being executed and was therefore not technically a soldier at all at the time of his death.

The dilemma of what to do with Miranda and the other executed men was solved by sending them to France. There was another American military cemetery in France, called Oise-Aisne American Cemetery and Memorial, and it too had a plot where those who had been executed were laid. Details of this may be found in Appendix 2. For the next 40 years Alex Miranda rested in peace. In 1988 a nephew of Miranda started a campaign to have his uncle's name cleared and for the finding of the court martial to be set aside on the grounds that he had not received a fair trial. Prejudice against him for his Hispanic origins was mentioned. In 1990, his remains were taken from Oise-Aisne American Cemetery and transported to California, where they were reburied in the Santa Ana cemetery in Orange County.

Chapter 13

Decline of the English Murder

On 15 February 1946 the left-wing magazine *Tribune* published an essay by George Orwell, who later became famous for books such as *Nineteen Eighty-Four* and *Animal Farm*. The piece, entitled 'Decline of the English Murder', lamented what Orwell saw as the end of the heyday of murder in England, as exemplified by cases such as Dr Crippen and Joseph Smith, the 'Brides in the Bath' killer. Orwell began by picturing an ordinary working man settling down after his Sunday lunch with the *News of the World* and becoming engrossed in some complex domestic tragedy which ended on the gallows. For George Orwell, the classic English murder had various common features. The murder had to take place in a purely domestic setting, for instance, and the participants had to be middle class. Sex was a vital element of the ideal murder and it also helped if nobody at first suspected that murder had been committed. This is why some of the classic murders, to Orwell's mind at least, involved poison.

After outlining what he saw as the ideal, traditional English murder, George Orwell compared and contrasted these with what he saw as the more commonplace and vulgar crimes of the 1940s, which he claimed were often a result of American influence, largely caused by the presence of so many American soldiers in the country during the Second World War. He cited the so-called 'Cleft Chin Murder' as exemplifying this trend and being a perfect specimen of the modern, Americanized murder. The 'Cleft Chin Murder' is of special interest in the context at which we have been looking, because it was the only case during the Second World War where an American soldier charged with murder was tried in a British court.

To understand how the 'Cleft Chin Murder' came about, we need to look first at the history of the two people responsible for it. These were a man and woman called Karl Hulten and Elizabeth Jones. Karl Gustav Hulten was born in Sweden in 1922 and when he was a child, he and his mother emigrated from there to the United States. Hulten grew up and went to school in Massachusetts and after leaving school, worked at a variety of dead-end jobs, which included being a driver, mechanic and shop assistant. Following the Japanese attack on Pearl Harbor in December 1941, he enlisted in the US Army. Although not yet 20 years of age, he was already married by that time and had a young child.

Elizabeth Maud Barker was from Glamorgan, a county in Wales. Born in 1926, she had what we would today call a troubled childhood. She truanted and her mother could not control her, although she was close to her father. When he was conscripted, Elizabeth tried to hitch-hike to the base where he was stationed. This was the last straw for her mother, who went to court to prove that her daughter was beyond her control. This resulted in the girl being sent to an approved school, which was a kind of residential industrial school for delinquents.

When she was released from the approved school at the age of 16, Elizabeth Barker promptly got married to a soldier called Stanley Jones, a man much older than her. The marriage lasted only a day as, according to Elizabeth, he was brutal to her on their wedding day. After this debacle, she took off for London, where she worked variously as a waitress, barmaid, cinema usherette and stripper, eking out a living as best she could. She had a foolish and romantic idea, probably caused by watching too many American films, that it would be exciting to be a gunman's 'moll'. In 1944, when she met up with Hulten, she was still only 18 years of age. She had by this time abandoned her own outstandingly prosaic name and was calling herself Georgina Grayson, which she felt had a touch of class about it.

While Jones was struggling to get by in London, Karl Hulten was finding that army life did not really suit him. He found it hard to adapt to the discipline and, just like Jones, had grandiose dreams of being somebody important. He stuck it out for as long as he could, but eventually he deserted, taking with him a 2½-ton army truck.

It was an unfortunate day that Hulten and Jones met. Sometimes, people have all manner of fantastic dreams and plans, which come to nothing and they settle down to the sort of humdrum life which most of us have. But when two people with such unrealistic and fanciful ideas team up, the consequences can be disastrous. There is a psychiatric syndrome known as *folie a deux* when two people might share a psychotic delusion, but a milder form of this may be seen when two people with foolish or dangerous ideas egg each other on and encourage one another to do things which they would never do if they were alone. This is what happened on Tuesday, 3 October 1944, when Elizabeth Jones was sitting in a café on Hammersmith Broadway in West London, drinking tea with a friend called Len Bexley. A good-looking young man in uniform walked in and Bexley introduced him to Jones as an acquaintance of his, a Lieutenant Rick Allen of the US Army. He was nothing of the sort, of course. In fact, he was none other than Karl Hulten, who was wearing a stolen uniform and, almost incredible, still driving around in the truck which he had stolen when he deserted from the army. We might observe in passing that when two people meet and both are using false names, any friendship between them is bound to be on a slightly peculiar footing. So it proved when the two young people encountered each other for the first time that day in the Black and White Café in Hammersmith.

Karl Hulten and Elizabeth Jones hit it off at once. He not only posed as an officer, but also claimed that he was in 'the Mob', in fact a gangster in Chicago. This was just what Jones had been looking for; a gunman whose 'moll' she might be. They arranged to meet that evening to go to the cinema. Even now, there was no reason why things should have progressed with quite the speed with which they did. Many inadequate people with strange daydreams meet up with each other without anything much happening. But there it was, Elizabeth Jones was thrilled to have met an American gangster and he for his part was probably hoping to impress her with his ferocity and daring.

'Ricky', as he insisted that Jones called him, did not turn up outside the Broadway Cinema at the appointed hour and the girl assumed that he had stood her up. Just as she began walking away, an enormous six-wheeled army lorry pulled up with 'Ricky' at the wheel. It is difficult to imagine a more conspicuous vehicle to ride around in, especially as it was stolen. The 'deuce and a half' or just plain 'deuce', referring to the load it could carry, used up a lot of fuel. Hulten had, with almost breath-taking effrontery, been filling it up for free at American bases, trusting that his officer's uniform would protect him from scrutiny. So far, he had been lucky. For six weeks he had cruised around in the lorry and never once been challenged.

Once Jones was sitting next to Hulten, they set off west, towards the town of Reading. On the way to Reading, the pair opened up a little and revealed both their true names and characters to each other. Karl Hulten admitted that he was no officer and that he was in fact a deserter. Jones in turn confessed that she was not quite the glamorous showgirl that she had led the American to believe, but that she was very keen to do something 'exciting', like be a real gangster's girlfriend. There was much debate at their later trial about which of them was the main driving force behind the notion of doing something 'exciting'. As is so often the case when such people are finally apprehended and brought to justice, both blamed the other. Perhaps it was a case of six of one and half a dozen of the other. In the event, their first bit of 'excitement' consisted of Hulten stopping the truck and then shoving a passing girl off her bicycle. She ran off in fear, leaving behind her handbag, which yielded less than a pound in loose change, along with some clothing coupons. It was a paltry beginning to a career of crime.

As they drove back to London, Karl Hulten revealed something else to the girl he was so intent upon impressing. This was that like any gangster worth his salt, he was carrying a gun, a US Army issue .45 calibre semi-automatic pistol, which he had stolen. The knowledge that her new boyfriend was armed was thrilling to Elizabeth Jones and she eagerly agreed to meet him again the following day, when perhaps they would share some more adventures. It must be borne in mind that she had only turned 18 two months earlier and was, to all intents and purposes, little more than an imaginative and slightly dull-witted child.

The day following their trip to Reading, Elizabeth Jones and her new boyfriend met up at 5:30 pm and went to see a film at the Hammersmith Gaumont. Afterwards, they went to a café and then set off once more towards Reading, with the vague idea of robbing a public house. We will never know which of the two was the more culpable in the events which took place over the next few days, because once arrested, it was only natural for the each of them to lay as much blame on the other as could be managed. At any rate, nothing came of the plan to raid the pub and as they headed back into London, one of them suggested holding a taxi driver up at gunpoint instead and stealing his takings. Unfortunately, the cab they chose happened to have a passenger in it who was inclined to resist any attempts at robbery. What's more, he was an American officer, a genuine one, and he had a gun of his own. Hulten and Jones beat a hasty retreat and made off in his lorry. There really was a touch of slapstick comedy about their efforts to become criminals, but this veered from comedy to tragedy very swiftly an hour later. After the abortive attempt on the taxi cab, they picked up a hitch-hiker, an 18-year-old girl called Violet May Hodge. Karl Hulten stopped the truck on the pretence of having a flat tyre and when the three of them got out of the vehicle, he struck her over the head with an iron bar, grabbed her handbag, rifled through her pockets and then pushed her into a nearby ditch. Violet Hodge survived this murderous assault, but it was no thanks to Karl Hulten and Elizabeth Jones. Again, their crime netted them only a trifling sum of money; five shillings, 25p in modern terms. After dropping Jones at her rented accommodation, the two agreed to meet once more the following evening and see if they could do any better.

On the evening of Friday, 6 October, Hulten and Jones decided that they would attack and rob a taxi driver. The American was armed with his automatic pistol. At about 11:00 pm that night, they hailed a cab in Hammersmith and asked the driver to take them towards Staines. The driver was 34-year-old George Heath and although reluctant to drive them all the way to Staines, he offered to take them as far as the Chiswick Roundabout, to which they agreed. When Heath stopped at Chiswick to let his passengers out of the car, Karl Hulten shot him in the back. The bullet smashed through his spine and paralysed him.

Both Hulten, who had actually fired the shot which struck the hapless taxi driver, and Jones, his willing accomplice, behaved with the utmost callousness after George Heath had been shot and wounded. Karl Hulten pushed him into the passenger seat and drove the car off towards Staines himself. On the way there, Jones went through the injured man's pockets, finding £8 in cash, along with a watch and a few other personal effects. At some point before they reached their destination, Heath died and when they arrived at Staines, Karl Hulten bundled the corpse out of the car and threw it in a ditch. Then they headed back to London.

Time was fast running out for the would-be gunman and his 'moll'. After stealing a car and killing the owner, the only sensible course of action would be to get rid of the car as soon as could be, but instead Karl Hulten drove around London in it, finding it perhaps a pleasant change from the heavy truck which he had been driving for the last month and a half. Inevitably, an alert police officer spotted the car and recognized the registration number, which had been circulated following the discovery of George Heath's body the day after he was murdered. Elizabeth Jones, far from being consumed by guilt, seemed to be revelling in what she and Hulten had done. She told a friend that if she had seen what Jones had seen, then she would not be able to sleep at night. By Monday, both man and woman were under arrest and soon charged with murder. Because of the distinctive appearance of their victim – Heath had a noticeable and pronounced cleft in his chin – the case became generally known as the 'Cleft Chin Murder'.

There was an immediate problem with how to try the two people allegedly involved in George Heath's murder. The contention of the police was that this was a case of what is known as 'joint enterprise'. This means that the two suspects were working together and that responsibility for the actions of one must be shared by the other. If two men burgle a house and one kills the occupant, both are guilty of murder. This principle still holds true in British law, of course. If two or more people are engaged in an unlawful enterprise and injury or death results, then all are equally guilty. Assuming this to be the case, then trying Hulten and Jones separately could end in an appalling miscarriage of justice. Suppose Hulten were to face a court martial and Jones an ordinary court. If he, who actually pulled the trigger, were acquitted, then Jones could still be found guilty. That could mean that the person who was merely present but did not shoot anybody could hang for murder, while her companion walked free. The only way to deal with the situation fairly and justly would be for both of the accused to be tried together in the same court. The United States ambassador, John G. Winant, who had helped hammer out the original deal granting immunity from British law of all American soldiers, reluctantly agreed that Karl Hulten could stand trial at London's Central Criminal Court, more commonly known as the Old Bailey. He was the first and only serviceman from the United States to face British justice in this way.

Karl Hulten and Elizabeth Jones both chose what is sometimes known in legal circles as a 'cutthroat defence'. That is to say both of them tried to lay all the blame for the crime on the other. Hulten said that Jones had urged him on and encouraged him to do things which he would not otherwise have dreamed of doing, while Jones claimed that she had been led along and was really no more than a spectator. As happens so often with this strategy, it ended with both the accused being found guilty.

From 16 January to 23 January 1945, the man and woman in the dock fought valiantly to persuade the jury that each was an innocent victim of the wiles of the other. Hulten's version of events was that

Elizabeth Jones had constantly been urging him on to do something 'exciting' and that the idea of robbing a taxi driver was hers alone. He had only gone along with the scheme because of the emotional hold she had over him. As for shooting George Heath, the gun had snagged on a strap as he brandished it at the driver and had gone off accidently. Jones, on the other hand, said that she had been terrified of Karl Hulten and did not dare try to leave him, as he had threatened to shoot her should she do so. At first she suggested that when she got in Heath's taxi, she was under the impression that Hulten had hailed it to take her home. Unfortunately, both defendants kept changing their stories, even as they were giving evidence, which did not give a very good impression to either judge or jury.

When the jury retired to consider their verdict on 23 January, after a conspicuously fair summing-up by the judge, Mr Justice Charles, there was very little doubt in the mind of most of those in court that day what they would decide. The only surprise really was how swiftly they came to a decision; they were out for just an hour and a half. Both Hulten and Jones were found guilty of murder, although the jury recommended mercy for the 18-year-old girl. When the traditional black cap was placed on the judge's head and he began to pronounce the death sentence, Elizabeth Jones went to pieces. As she was led back to the cells, she shrieked, 'Oh! Why didn't he tell the truth?'

It might have been expected that sympathy would be felt for a teenage girl facing the prospect of being hanged, but in fact there was a good deal of hostility towards Jones, even in her home town of Neath. It was believed that the jury's recommendation for mercy might mean that she would be reprieved. Graffiti appeared in Neath, chalked on walls. This consisted of a gallows, with the caption beneath it saying, 'She should hang'. This began to look increasingly likely, following the rejection in February of appeals from both Hulten and Jones.

The American ambassador sought, and was granted, an interview with the Home Secretary, whose unenviable job it was to decide whether either or both of the convicted murderers should hang. It was within Herbert Morrison's gift to recommend that the sentence of death should be set aside and replaced with imprisonment for life. After their appeal had failed, an execution date had been set for Karl Hulten and Elizabeth Jones. They were both to hang on the morning of 8 March 1945. What the ambassador wished to be assured of was that if one were to hang, then both would. He spent almost an hour trying to persuade the Home Secretary that it would be grossly unfair if only the American should be hanged. The two of them had been convicted of murder and therefore either both or neither should be executed.

Making a decision about the merits of a reprieve for the murderers in the 'Cleft Chin Murder' case was not easy and Herbert Morrison left it until the last possible moment. In the end, it was Elizabeth Jones' age and gender which saved her life. Only eleven women had been hanged in Britain so far that century and not since Queen Victoria was on the throne had a teenage girl been executed. No such considerations applied in the case of Karl Hulten though, and the American ambassador's pleas were in vain. On 6 March, just 48 hours before the executions were scheduled to take place, Hulten and Jones were informed of their respective fates.

When the governor of Holloway Prison told Elizabeth Jones that she had been granted a reprieve, the girl understood it to mean that she was to be freed. She asked if she could write to her mother, so that her best clothes could be brought to the prison for when she walked out of the gates. She said too that her mother would very likely want to arrange for a homecoming party for her. When the governor explained that instead of being released at once, her sentence was one of life imprisonment and that she could expect to spend at least 10 or 12 years in prison, Jones became hysterical and had to be sedated and taken to the prison hospital. It all went to show the shallowness of her personality which was, whatever she had done, still that of an immature child, rather than a grown woman. She did not seem at all grateful for having her life preserved, for in one of the first letters she wrote after being reprieved, she said, 'I would rather die than serve a prison sentence. God-what a jury! How I hate the London people. Hate them like poison.' In the event, she served just nine years in prison, being released early in 1954, when she was still only 27. She had no income and so sold her life story to one of the more sensational of the Sunday newspapers.

As for Karl Hulten, he converted to Catholicism in the condemned cell. This was the religion of the woman he had married. On the morning of Thursday, 8 March, he kept his appointment with Tom Pierrepoint, the same man who would have hanged him had he been sentenced to death by an American court martial. He was executed just five days before his 23rd birthday.

In 1990 a film based upon this case was released. It was called *Chicago Joe and the Showgirl* and starred Kiefer Sutherland and Emily Lloyd.

Chapter 14

The Last Firing Squad in England

For centuries, the British tried to ensure that firing squads did not operate in their country. They have had no difficulty shooting people ceremonially abroad, but the crash of rifles ending some unfortunate person's life was somehow felt not to be quite the thing in England itself. During the unrest in Scotland in 1743, a Highland regiment stationed in London mutinied and three of the ringleaders were shot at the Tower of London. An eighteenth-century map of London shows that near to Tyburn, where hangings were carried out in London, close to the modern site of Marble Arch, a field is marked as, 'Where soldier are shot'. After the eighteenth century though, nobody else was executed in this way on the British mainland until the First World War. Even then, only foreigners were shot. British soldiers who were to be executed for cowardice or desertion were all shot in France. Even if they had managed to get back to Britain after deserting from the Western Front, they were shipped back there to be executed.

Eight people were shot by firing squad during the First World War, but these were all German spies. They had faced courts martial when captured and it was thought that they deserved a more honourable death than hanging. All were shot at the Tower of London. Only one spy was hanged during that war. The British cheerfully executed people in this way in any country in which their army operated; it was only in Britain itself that they tried to avoid executions of this kind. In Singapore, for instance, the British dealt with a mutiny by an Indian unit, the 5th (Native) Light Infantry, by means of one of the largest firing squads in history. On 23 February 1915, 21 of the Indian mutineers were lined up against a wall and shot by 105 British soldiers.

By the time of the Second World War, nobody seriously expected to see another firing squad being used to execute a prisoner in Britain. Captured spies were being hanged, rather than shot. There was one exception to this general rule, a German meteorologist called Josef Jakobs, who was a sergeant in the Wehrmacht.

On 31 January 1941, Sergeant Jakobs was parachuted into England from a Luftwaffe plane. He was wearing civilian clothes, which immediately removed all protection from the Geneva Convention. He was bound to be treated as a spy if caught. Things went wrong quite literally as soon as he landed. The 43-year-old soldier broke his ankle as he hit the ground. Since he could no longer walk, he was obliged to summon help by firing his pistol into the air. When he was charged under the Treachery Act 1940, Josef Jakobs' anxiety centred around one point in particular. He must have known perfectly well that he was very likely to face execution for his actions, but it was the mode of death which worried him, rather than its inevitability. He asked the man who read the charge to him, Lieutenant Colonel Cooke, what would happen to him if he were to be convicted. Cooke told him that as a serving soldier he would face a court martial, rather than a civilian court, and that if found guilty he would be shot. It seemed a weight off Jakobs' mind to learn this. 'Honourable death by powder and shot' he could face, but the prospect of being hanged was unendurable to him. On 15 August that same year, Josef Jakobs was executed at the Tower of London by an army firing squad.

It was widely assumed after Jakobs' death that this was likely to be the last such execution carried out in Britain. Certainly, all the other spies and traitors were hanged. But of course, there were to be two more firing squads operating in Britain and this is the story of the last execution by this method ever performed in the country.

In the spring of 1942, a contingent of American soldiers arrived in the Wiltshire town of Westbury with the task of building the Central Ordnance Supply Depot. This was really an arms dump, where weaponry would be stored and distributed to other units. Although the Americans have been gone for many decades, some of the street names in the area, now occupied by a sprawling trading estate, still bear witness to those who were once quartered here; Broadway, Main Street and Washington Road. Because the US Army was segregated at that time and there would be black and white units stationed in the town, other properties were allocated to be used as barracks for black soldiers, among them Fontaineville House in Edward Street and the Drill Hall in West End. Two of the men stationed in the Drill Hall were Benjamin Pyegate and James Alexander.

On the evening of 17 June 1944, a number of the soldiers stationed in and around the Drill Hall were drinking beer in the recreation hall which had been established in the building. Barrack huts had been erected around the Drill Hall, which acted as the nucleus of the complex. The hall had previously been used by the Territorial Army, peacetime reserves of the British army. On this particular evening, 35-year-old Pyegate arrived at the recreation hall just as the bar was closing. He was irritated, because it meant that he was unable to have a drink. Indeed, to say that he was irritated is perhaps to understate the case. He said to the man who was dispensing the beer, 'If I come in again and can't get any beer, I will turn the place out'. He then had an argument with a man called Dempsey, in the course of which another soldier called Easley joined in on Dempsey's side. The other soldiers in his hut had been drinking freely, for it was a Saturday night and a certain amount of freedom was allowed at weekends. The amount of alcohol which had been consumed by other soldiers might possibly have a bearing on what happened after the bar closed and the men drifted back to their huts. From what transpired, it is clear that some of those who had been drinking that night were expecting trouble.

Dempsey and Easley were staying in the same hut as James Alexander, who had taken no part in the argument. After these three men had gone into the hut where they were sleeping, a group of other men, including Pyegate, gathered outside, shouting angrily. Dempsey, Easley and James Alexander came out of the hut. Easley was holding a bottle behind his back and Dempsey had a poker in his hand. They later said that they felt threatened. Alexander had not armed himself and tried to calm things down. This seemed to annoy Benjamin Pyegate, who told him, 'Get back in that hut before I kill you!' It was no idle threat. Pyegate moved forward and snatched the bottle from Easley. After he had done so, he lashed out with his boot, catching James Alexander in the groin. As the man he had kicked doubled up in pain, Pyegate pulled out a knife and plunged it into Alexander's neck, cutting his throat and causing the man to choke to death on his own blood.

It is hard to imagine a more clear-cut case of murder. A man takes out a knife and then stabs another man in the throat, who then dies, all this in front of various witnesses. It comes as no surprise to learn that within a matter of hours, Benjamin Pyegate had been charged as follows;

> Violation of the 92nd Article of War. Specification: In that Private Benjamin Pyegate 950th Quartermaster Service Company at Drill Hall Camp, Westbury, Wiltshire, England, on or about 17th June 1944, with malice aforethought, wilfully, deliberately, feloniously, unlawfully and with premeditation, did kill Private First Class James Alexander, a human being, by stabbing him in the throat with a knife.

Justice moved very swiftly at that time, as has already been remarked, and just a month later, on 15 July, Pyegate faced a court martial.

Although he pleaded not guilty to the charge, Benjamin Pyegate's defence was extremely weak, although what it lacked in strength, it more than made up for in ingenuity. It was as follows. On 25 April 1944, a heavy box had fallen on Pyegate's head, causing a wound which required stitches. There was no doubt about this, for at his trial a Captain George Schwartz of the Medical Corps testified that he had treated Pyegate for this injury, putting ten stitches in the cut. In his opinion though, this was a superficial cut which was very unlikely to have caused any damage to the man's brain. Benjamin Pyegate's contention was that ever since this injury, he had suffered from blackouts and spells of amnesia. It was a good scheme, because if he genuinely could not recollect that incident for which he was being tried, then it would be against the principles of natural justice to punish him. His statement about the events of that tragic evening ran as follows.

According to Pyegate, he had tried to calm matters down outside the hut by saying that, 'You fellows are all in the same company, and you should be friends'. He saw that one man was holding a bottle, which he took from him. That was the last thing he remembered, for his amnesia now struck and he did not come to again until he was back at his own hut. He had a hazy memory of going to the latrine in his hut and then being ordered to come with an officer. He denied ever possessing a knife since he had joined the army and was unable to shed any light at all on the murder of James Alexander.

There was no evidence really of any history of amnesia and the first that anybody had heard of the injury to his skull causing these mental effects was when he found himself on trial for murder. It was certainly not the view of the case which the court was inclined to adopt and Pyegate was convicted of the killing and sentenced to death. The crime did not involve the civilian population and took place on an American base and so it was decided that the condemned man should face a firing squad, rather than the gallows. The justification for making such a decision is slender enough, but there it was.

We saw in an earlier chapter that following the last civilian execution at Shepton Mallet, in 1926, there were persistent and widespread rumours that the sound of the execution, specifically the boom as the trapdoors fell, could be heard in the streets around the prison. It was necessary for the Home Secretary himself to squash that story. Much the same thing had happened after the execution by firing squad of Alex Miranda in May 1944. There may have been some question as to whether the banging of the trapdoors of the gallows might have been audible outside the confines of the prison, but there was no debate about the crash of rifle fire being clearly heard across the whole town when Miranda was executed. Many people in Shepton Mallet objected strongly to being compelled in this way to witness an execution and representations were made to the US Army on the subject. A cunning scheme was hit upon. It was decided to hold the execution at precisely 8:00 am. Several church clocks chimed at that hour and, it was hoped, they would serve to drown out the sound of seven rifles being fired simultaneously.

On the morning of 28 November, Benjamin Pyegate was brought to the wall shown in Illustration 16. Sandbags had been piled up behind the post which had been erected and he was tied to this with leather straps and a hood placed over his head. As the church clocks of Shepton Mallet began to chime eight o'clock, the order was given to fire and seven bullets smashed into Pyegate's chest. It was not necessary for a *coup de grace* to be delivered with a pistol shot to the head, as sometimes happened with such executions.

The sound of the gunfire had, despite the precautions, been audible to people in and around the prison and this was the last time that a firing squad was used in the prison yard at Shepton Mallet or indeed, ever again anywhere in Britain.

Chapter 15

The Last Execution at Shepton Mallet

T he last execution to be carried out at Shepton Mallet Prison was, coincidentally, also the last for rape in Britain. The last person to be hanged for rape in England was Richard Smith, at Nottingham on 30 March 1836. A few years later the law was changed and rape ceased to be a capital offence. For the next century or so, it must have seemed exceedingly improbably that anybody would ever again suffer the supreme penalty in Britain for rape alone, unaccompanied by murder. The case was of course wholly altered when the US Army arrived in the country in 1942.

We have already looked at rapes which resulted in soldiers being hanged at Shepton Mallet. The last such instance is in some ways the worst of all and it is difficult to summon up much sympathy for the man who was hanged, however much we may in principle disapprove of the death penalty.

In August 1944 22-year-old Aniceto Martinez, who was from New Mexico, was a guard at a prisoner of war camp at Rugeley, in the English county of Staffordshire. On the night of Saturday, 5 August, Martinez went drinking in Rugeley visiting, by his own account, two or three public houses. In his own words, he 'was not drunk, but was feeling high'. One of the pubs which he visited was the Crown Inn, which is a short distance from a road called Sandy Lane. After the pubs closed, Martinez wandered around for a while, apparently going to the house of somebody he knew in the area, but who was not at home. Eventually, at about 3:00 am, he found himself in Sandy Lane. According to his sworn statement, which was read out at the subsequent court martial, an acquaintance had told Martinez that 15 Sandy Lane was what he termed quaintly, 'a house of ill repute', in other words, a brothel.

Martinez said in his statement, after being arrested, that he had seen a number of women in the house previously and also seen soldiers going in and out. On questioning though, he admitted that he could not be sure that the house he was thinking of was actually No. 15. It could have been 18 or 19. Finding that there were no lights on in the house and being apparently desperate for sex, he kicked down the back door to gain entrance to the property.

Far from being a brothel, 15 Sandy Lane was in fact the home of a 75-year-old widow called Agnes Cope, who lived alone. She mentioned at the trial that she had lived in the house for 43 years, since the relief of Mafeking, during the Boer War. There was a reason that she was asked about the length of time that she had been in the house, as we shall later see. Mrs Cope woke up at 3:15 am to find an intruder in her bedroom. She told the police that she said to the man, 'Oh master, whatever do you want? If it is money you want, I do not have any.' Martinez told her that it was not money he wanted, but a woman. She was able to be so sure about the time of the attack because Martinez had picked up the alarm clock from a table at the side of the bed and told her, 'It's a quarter past three, missus.' She could tell by now that he had an American accent and was dressed in uniform. The man in her bedroom now tried to force himself on her sexually. When she showed signs of resistance, he struck her and continued to hit her every time she cried out or attempted to stop him from raping her. After the man had left, Agnes Cope was too terrified to leave the room or raise the alarm. It was not until her daughter came to the house that morning that the old woman was able to tell anybody what had happened. The police surgeon who examined her noted that she had a black eye, various bruises and a sprained thumb. It was, by any standards, a shocking crime to be committed against a defenceless old woman and the police were very swift to track down the culprit.

Inspector Horace Brookes went to the house in Sandy Lane and found that the back door had been forced open. He found too the impression where somebody had apparently laid full length in a flower bed and vomited. Since the man who had committed this dreadful crime was an American, he went that afternoon to the nearest place where American soldiers were stationed in Rugeley, which was the Flaxley Green Camp in Stilecop Field. This was a prisoner of war camp holding Italians. There were six compounds for prisoners and one for the men guarding them. Once he had spoken to the officer in charge, it did not take very long to find which of the soldiers had been responsible for the ordeal suffered by Agnes Cope. One man alone had been absent from his bed when a routine check had been carried out the previous night. Aniceto Martinez claimed that he had fallen asleep in the latrine, which was why he had not been in his bed, but there was a very strong suspicion that this was a lie. Although of course he had no power to arrest the man, the officers at Flaxley Green were as disgusted by the crime as everybody else who had heard about it. They willingly allowed the British police to take away Martinez' uniform for analysis. In the meantime, the suspected man was kept under guard.

It did not take long for the Midland Forensic Laboratory in Gooch Street North, Birmingham, to come up with its findings. On Martinez's cap was found both a thorn which matched the hedge behind Mrs Cope's house and also blue threads matching those from the quilt on her bed. White threads, matching the old woman's nightdress, were found tangled around his trouser buttons. There could hardly have been a more damning collection of evidence. Before this evidence came back though, Aniceto Martinez decided that the best thing to do was make one or two admissions and mix them with stout denials. He agreed that he had been in the house and even in the bedroom, and made a statement, in which he said,

> I did go into the house but I did not break the door down, I did commit misconduct with a woman but she was not forced. It was at a little house at the bottom of a hill near the pub. It happened last night. I had some drink, but I was not drunk. I was sick near the house.

Having made these damning admissions, Martinez said, 'I refuse to sign that statement and then you can't use it against me at a court martial.' Those questioning him were left with the impression that he was perhaps hinting that Agnes Cope was a prostitute, who had willingly agreed to have sex with the young soldier. This tied in neatly with the story that he told of having been led to believe that 15 Sandy Lane was a brothel, an idea which he later enlarged upon when questioned by an American officer, Lieutenant Ford on the Monday following his arrest.

Martinez told Lieutenant Ford that the whole reason for his going to Agnes Cope's house was that it was well known to be a brothel. His statement about this is worth quoting at length, because it was the main plank in his defence when he was court-martialled.

> About six o'clock I went into Rugeley and called at several pubs. I ended up in the Crown Hotel at closing time. I left there and walked towards the camp, and when I got to the crossroads turned right as I was supposed to go to a house to visit friends. I saw the house was in darkness so turned around and went back. I had had some drinks but was not drunk, was just feeling high. I got to a group of houses on the right-hand side where I had had a few words with a lady living in one of the houses on two occasions, and went to the house where I thought she lived. I knocked but no one answered, so I turned the knob and walked in. I went upstairs and the lady asked me if I wanted money. I told her it was not money, and then pulled her down on the bed. After leaving the house I went back to the camp, but did not sign in. I went to sleep in a latrine and later went to my bunk.

There seemed on the face of it very meagre material here upon which to base any defence, but the officers assigned to represent Martinez at the court martial, Captain Dolezal and Captain Winthaub, who had that unenviable task, did the best they could.

Because of events in Europe, the Normandy landings having taken place only two months earlier, it was to be some time before Martinez faced the inevitable court martial. It was not until February 1945 that he appeared for his trial. The prosecution had a formidable array of evidence and was prepared to counter anything which the defence might try and spring upon them. Aniceto Martinez chose to stake everything upon the feeble idea that he had mistaken Mrs Cope's house for a brothel. In a sworn statement which he presented to the court, he expanded upon this idea. He claimed that when he was speaking to a civilian outside the YMCA, the house in Sandy Lane had been pointed out to him as somewhere he could 'get fixed up' if he wanted sex. He said that he and some other soldiers had gone to the house and a woman had answered the door and told them to come back another time. The next time he passed the place, he said that there was a group of soldiers outside and that the Military Police had told him to move along.

The thrust of the defence put forward by Martinez was that he honestly thought that 15 Sandy Lane was a brothel and that it was simply a case of genuine confusion on his part. It was for this reason that the prosecution drew out of the victim when she gave evidence that she had lived at the house since the Boer War and that there was no possible chance of anybody having run a brothel there.

The defending officers then drew attention to the fact that Martinez was not very highly educated, as though that were somehow a mitigating factor. It can have come as no surprise to anybody, except perhaps the defendant, when after a short adjournment, the court found Martinez guilty of rape, in violation of the 24th Article of War. There were only two possible sentences for such an offence, either death or imprisonment for life. The sentence chosen was death, but this depended upon the recommendations of higher authorities. All death sentences needed to be confirmed by the Supreme Commander of the Allied Forces, General Eisenhower.

Confirmation of the sentence took a long time to come, because of course the US Army and its generals had other, more urgent matters to attend to in the spring of 1945, such as defeating Nazi Germany. All these delays in both bringing the case to trial and then confirming the verdict and sentence of the court gave Aniceto Martinez almost another year of life. The rape had been committed in August 1944 and it was not until June 1945 that the end of the case was finally reached. At one o'clock in the morning of 15 June 1945 Aniceto Martinez was hanged by Tom Pierrepoint, aided by his nephew Albert. This was to be the last execution ever carried out at Shepton Mallet Prison and the also the last for rape in Britain.

In the next chapter we shall be asking ourselves if it was worth the British making so much fuss about ensuring that their own hangman carried out the executions at Shepton Mallet. Might it be the case that it would have made no real difference if the Americans had been left to arrange matters in their own way?

Chapter 16

American Military Executions
at Nuremberg

We have looked in considerable detail at the process used in Britain for ensuring that executioners were of good character, unlikely to be drunkards, and were all properly and comprehensively trained in the most up-to-date methods of hanging people painlessly and efficiently. These precautions meant that in all but one or two cases, every hanging carried out in the country over the course of the twentieth century resulted in a neatly broken neck. The exceptions were when the prisoner had fainted at the last moment and so the trapdoor was opened as the person slumped down. This meant that the full drop was not given and as a consequence, the victim was strangled, rather than dying of a broken neck. Even this extremely rare mishap was obviated from the 1920s onwards by the simple expedient of having prison officers stand either side of the man or woman to be executed, holding their arms, so that if there was a last-minute fainting fit, the person to be hanged would still be kept upright and receive the recommended drop.

Perhaps though, everything would have gone pretty well as smoothly, had the Americans instead have chosen a hangman of their own and allowed him to undertake those executions at Shepton Mallet? Could it be that the British were being needlessly fussy about who actually put the rope around the men's necks and pulled the lever? To answer this question we must look at what happened after the invasion of France in 1944 by the British and US Armies. It was rightly guessed that there were likely to be more courts martial held at a time when fighting was actually taking place in an area, than when men were simply stationed in a country on the edge of occupied territory. For this reason, it was decided to recruit an American executioner, one able to carry out hangings in Europe as the US Army advanced on Germany.

A few hangings of American servicemen outside Britain had already taken place before the Normandy landings. These were carried out in the Algerian town of Oran, the island of Sicily and on the Italian mainland. The army though needed a man stationed in France after the invasion, so that he could be on hand to conduct any hangings ordered by courts martial.

There was to be no painstaking care in finding a man to hang people during the later stages of the greatest war ever seen; the Americans were in something of a hurry. With the chaos in Europe, murders and rapes were sure to be committed before long by some of the soldiers fighting for the United States and so there was a sense of urgency about arranging for an executioner to be standing by, ready for the first sentence of death to be pronounced and confirmed. Word was circulated among the American armed forces in Europe that an executioner was needed, specifically, a man who had previous experience of carrying out hangings. It did not take long for a volunteer to appear.

Private John C. Woods belonged to the 37th Engineer Combat Battalion of the 5th Engineer Special Brigade. His unit had landed in France as part of the invasion force launched on D–Day, although he had not himself taken part in any fighting. He claimed to have assisted, before the war, at hangings in Texas and Oklahoma. The army took him at his word and he was promoted to Master Sergeant. Woods was then transferred from the combat unit in which he was serving and attached to the 2913th Disciplinary Training Center in Paris. He was at this time 33 years of age.

Before going any further, it must be noted that John Woods was perhaps not the ideal man to appoint as hangman. Something which the army did not know at that time was that he had previously been dishonourably discharged from the US Navy 14 years earlier, after enlisting and then going absent without leave a few months later. A psychiatric evaluation conducted before he was discharged concluded that Woods was an inadequate psychopath. It is doubtful if he had any previous experience of hangings either and it is most likely that his offer to act as executioner was prompted by simple motives of self-interest. For one thing, being a member of the Disciplinary Center would have the effect of removing him from the danger inherent in serving in a war zone. For another, the promotion which his appointment secured had the effect of almost tripling his pay, from the $50 a month earned by a private to $138 as a master sergeant.

The basic principle of hanging is of course easy enough to grasp. If you suspend a man by means of a rope around his neck, he is sure to die sooner or later. Drop him through the air for 6ft and there is a reasonable chance that he will be killed at once by a broken neck. Either way, whether your victim chokes to death over the course of half an hour, which was certainly the fate of some of Woods' victims, or has his neck snapped by the drop, he will eventually die as a result of your actions. This was the principle upon which John Woods, a man who had never actually hanged anybody before in his life, worked for the next few years.

To be fair to Woods, despite his complete lack of either theoretical or practical knowledge regarding executions by hanging, he was probably no worse at the business than the average hangman operating outside the United Kingdom. In that country, the process of hanging had been perfected until it was almost an art, but most other countries did not trouble too much about the finer points or technicalities of the thing. As long as the condemned criminal ended up hanging on the end of the rope, dead, that was quite sufficient. And if there is one thing certain, it is that hanging a man or woman by the neck for long enough will surely result in death!

The most commonly seen photograph of John C. Woods is reproduced here as Illustration 19. He is, perhaps inevitably, holding a classic, 'cowboy coil' type of noose. This is the kind of noose which he used for every execution which he undertook. He also adhered to the time-honoured American practice of the fixed drop. Everybody he hanged received the same, unvarying, 6ft drop, when once the trapdoors upon which they were standing opened beneath their feet. Woods did not seem to grasp the crucial importance of the positioning of the knot when hanging a man. He seemed to place the rope more or less randomly around the neck of the men he hanged, not paying any attention to whether the knot was under one ear or another, or even if it was at the back of the neck when the hanging was carried out. This too introduced an element of surprise into executions, for it was never possible to predict whether or not the man being hanged would die instantly or need Woods to go below the scaffold to swing on his legs, as had been the custom in Britain in the eighteenth and early nineteenth centuries. This was actually witnessed at one of the executions which Woods carried out, two years after he was officially appointed the American army's executioner in October 1944.

We have looked closely at the background of John C. Woods, because it sheds light on what might have been the fate of those men executed at Shepton Mallet, had the British not stood firm on the question of who would actually conduct the hangings on their soil. We are fortunate enough to have several detailed accounts of how Woods dealt with his victims, because in addition to hanging three dozen American soldiers in 1944 and 1945, he also hanged almost fifty German war criminals, including all the most famous soldiers and political leaders of the Third Reich who were found guilty of war crimes at the Nuremberg trials in 1946. A number of newspaper reporters witnessed these, the most important of the executions which Woods undertook, and they give us an insight into his *modus operandi*.

There was already some unease about John Woods' abilities as a hangman by the time that the Nuremberg trials began in November 1945. It was observed that some of his victims 'died hard', as the old saying had it. In short, they were strangled, rather than having their necks cleanly snapped. There was though a certain amount of national prestige involved in choosing which country's executioner should have the honour of ending the lives of some of the most notorious criminals of the twentieth century. As the senior partner in the coalition which had invaded Europe and brought the Nazi regime to an end, it was perhaps inevitable that the United States would have the final say in the matter and they were determined that their own man would hang such famous individuals as Von Ribbentrop and Hermann Göring, once the formality of the trial had been concluded. In the event, of course, Göring, perhaps the most notorious of the men on trial, succeeded in anticipating the sentence pronounced by the court and poisoning himself the night before his scheduled execution. The execution of the remaining ten prominent Nazis gave the entire world the opportunity to observe closely the American method of hanging. It was a gruesome display which fully justified the decision made four years earlier to forbid any American-style hangings in Britain.

The execution of the first of the Nazi war criminals took place in the gymnasium of Nuremberg Prison in the early hours of 16 October 1946. Three sets of gallows had been erected side by side, in order to speed up the pace of the executions which were to take place. The plan was that one man would be hanged on the first gallows and while his body was still suspended, the next victim would be brought out and hanged on the second gallows. By the time the third man had dropped through the trapdoors, the first man to be hanged would presumably be dead and the body ready to be removed, freeing up this gallows for the next customer. It was like some ghastly conveyor-belt system or production line of death. As Woods remarked, with almost inconceivable bad taste, after hanging the ten men, 'Ten men in 103 minutes. That's fast work!'

Perhaps the work was too fast to be efficient, because it was apparent to the assembled witnesses that things were not proceeding as smoothly as might have been hoped. The first of the Nazi leaders to be hanged by Master Sergeant Woods was Joachim von Ribbentrop, formerly the German Foreign Minister. Woods was working with a member of the Military Police called Joseph Malta and the two of them fastened Von Ribbentrop's hands behind his back and, when he was positioned on the scaffold, strapped his legs together with an army-issue webbing belt. He then plummeted through the trapdoor, but he was not killed immediately. The drop stunned him, but he took 14 minutes to choke to death. The rope was still quivering with his struggles when the next victim, Field Marshal Wilhelm Keitel, was led up the steps of the adjacent gallows. After saying a few last words, Keitel too was hanged, but his death was even harder than Von Ribbentrop's. As he fell through the trapdoor, his face struck the rebounding trapdoor, cutting it open. He took almost half an hour to die as could be seen from the fact that the rope was moving and shaking for this length of time. When his corpse was later displayed to the assembled witnesses, it was seen that his face was covered in blood from the injuries received during execution.

One journalist who was present at the executions carried out by Woods was Joseph Kingsbury-Smith and he wrote a detailed account of the terrible bungling. Of the hanging of Julius Streicher, editor of a virulently anti-Semitic newspaper in the 1930s and a close friend of Hitler, Kingsbury-Smith recorded the following;

> When the rope snapped taut with the body swinging wildly, groans could be heard from within the concealed interior of the scaffold. Finally, the hangman, who had descended from the gallows platform, lifted the black canvas curtain and went inside. Something happened that put a stop to the groans and brought the rope to a standstill. After it was over, I was not in the mood to ask what he did, but I assume that he grabbed the swinging body and pulled down on it. We were all of the opinion that Streicher had strangled.

Woods himself admitted later that some of the men he had hanged kicked for a while on the end of the rope, which certainly indicates that they had not died instantly from broken necks.

The ten corpses of those executed that night were laid out with the ropes still around their necks and witnesses were allowed to file past and examine them. Photographs were also taken, to avoid any later suggestion that the Nazi leaders had escaped justice and were still alive. It was plain that in several cases, the executed men had suffered facial injuries in addition to being strangled. The American army indignantly denied that any of the men hanged on this occasion had been choked to death, claiming that all had died speedily of broken necks. However, within a matter of hours, the corpses had been taken to Munich and cremated, the ashes later being scattered in a river, to prevent the remains becoming the focus of neo-Nazi pilgrimage. Because of this, there is no way of ever confirming the actual cause of death. No autopsies were conducted: it was enough for a doctor to certify death.

Executions by hanging were still being carried out in the United States until 1996 and although some parts of the procedure were modified and improved, other aspects remained unchanged. For example, a table of different drops, calculated according to the weight of the condemned person was introduced and this certainly increased the chances that the victim would die of a broken neck. However, the traditional 'cowboy coil' noose was still used for the last hanging ever to take place in America, that of Billy Bailey, on 25 January 1996.

In this chapter we have looked in gruesome detail at the American way of hanging men in the 1940s and seen just why the British authorities were not minded to allow anything similar to take place in their own country. Whatever our views on the death penalty, almost everybody agrees that if it is to be inflicted, then it should be done with as little suffering and pain on the part of the condemned person as is humanly possible. By 1942 the British had spent a century or so making every conceivable improvement to executing people by hanging. Albert Pierrepoint, perhaps the most famous British hangman of all time, once entered the condemned cell and seven seconds later the occupant of the cell was hanging dead on the end of the rope. It was this unrivalled speed and efficiency which the authorities in London wished to see applied to any hanging which took place in their country.

Chapter 17

The End of American Jurisdiction in Britain?

W e have seen throughout this book that the United States has, from its very inception, been hugely reluctant to allow other nations to dictate what either the US itself should be obliged to do or to allow its citizens to be put on trial by any other country. The only terms on which they agreed to enter the Second World War were that they should not be bound by a formal alliance and that no other nation, not even their staunchest friend, Britain, should be allowed to prosecute and bring to trial any of its servicemen, for any reason whatsoever. One would hope that a measure such as the one which prevented the British police or courts from taking any action against American soldiers or airmen would be no more today than an historical curiosity, but recent events do cause us to wonder. The case mentioned in an earlier chapter, the death of Harry Dunn in 2019, brought to light some intriguing evidence that things haven't really changed all that much in this respect since the end of the Second World War in 1945.

The law which granted immunity to American servicemen in the United Kingdom lingered on until seven years after the end of the Second World War. It was eventually replaced with a broader law covering men and women serving with Commonwealth forces stationed in or visiting Britain, together with the forces of any other nation that might be added to the provisions of this act. This was the Visiting Forces Act 1952. Those chiefly affected by this act were United States airmen stationed in Britain. From the end of the Second World War until the early 1990s, America had a number of air bases in Britain. Foreign soldiers who fell under the Visiting Forces Act were, in general, answerable to British courts for offences committed on British soil, although there were one or two loopholes which the Americans were not slow to exploit. One of these was that soldiers who fell within the scope of the act could not be held accountable to the British courts for anything at all they did in the course of their military duty, not unless their country agreed. This really was an extraordinary concession for the British to make and it has been the subject of some controversy. Who decided if the people accused of offences were acting in the course of their duty? That would be the senior officers of the country concerned.

To see how the Visiting Forces Act worked to the advantage of America, we need only look at one or two specific cases. The reason that this act really only affected American airmen is not hard to see. Although it theoretically applied equally to soldiers from Cyprus or Zambia, such troops have never been commonly seen in the United Kingdom. The chances of a Zimbabwean soldier killing anybody while on military duty in the United Kingdom have always been vanishingly slender, but given the large number of American servicemen in the country over the years, the occasional accidental death or murder was bound to be seen from time to time. When it did happen, the United States was very quick off the mark to make sure that it was they who dealt with the matter, rather than the British judicial system. Take, for instance, a case in 1979 which has eerie similarities to that of Harry Dunn, which was to cause a great deal of fuss 40 years later.

In August 1979 a US Marine who was working as a guard at a nuclear weapons store in the RAF base at St Mawgan, in Cornwall, was driving at great speed along the wrong side of the road. He killed a 17-year-old youth and was facing prosecution. The American authorities though declared that he was driving in pursuit of his military duties and that the incident thus fell under their jurisdiction, rather than that of the British courts. They had a perfect right to do this, although it caused some raised eyebrows in Britain. Incredibly, at his court martial, the man was fined just $1 for causing the death.

Of course, the American forces did not always have it all their own way and in one notorious case, their failure to browbeat the British into allowing them jurisdiction in a case of murder actually worked to the advantage of the accused man. I shall begin by setting out bluntly what was done by an American airman on New Year's Eve 1960 and then we shall see how the case played out when once he was apprehended by the British police.

At the end of 1960, 29-year-old Willis Eugene Boshears was a staff sergeant at the Wethersfield US Air Force Base near Dunmow in Essex. He was married to a Scots woman who had gone to spend Christmas with her parents in Scotland. Boshears was accordingly spending Christmas and the New Year alone in the flat in which they lived. On the evening of Saturday, 31 December 1960 Willie Boshears went to a local pub. There he met a 20-year-old girl whom he knew, called Jean Constable. At the end of the evening he invited her and an Englishman called David Sault back to his flat, so that they could carry on drinking there.

David Sault left Boshears' flat a few hours after arriving, but Jean Constable remained. Shortly after Sault went, Willie Boshears strangled the young woman and then later, in a bid to disguise her body, cut off all her long brown hair. He burned this in the hearth, along with her distinctive coat, handbag and various other items of her clothing. He took a ring which she had been wearing and threw it away, although he kept the money from her handbag and also the watch which she had on. Then he stripped the corpse naked and washed it thoroughly in the bath in an effort to remove any forensic evidence. Two days later, he put the dead body in his car and drove a few miles into the countryside, before dumping it in a ditch. Jean Constable had been seen speaking to a number of airmen from the Wethersfield base on the evening she died and it had not proved difficult to track down the taxi driver who had picked up her and the two men and taken them to Boshears' flat. When the corpse of the young woman was discovered and the police began making enquiries, it was not long before they found their way to Boshears. He was charged with Jean Constable's murder.

Up to this point there seems nothing to distinguish this crime for a hundred other sordid affairs of a similar type. There was something monstrously cold-blooded about the way that he cut the hair from the dead girl's head and then threw her in a ditch like a piece of discarded rubbish. There was no dispute about what he had done; he freely admitted it all during the police interview and confirmed what he had said when he appeared in court. Matters then took two startling turns. The first came when Boshears appeared in the magistrates' court after being charged with murder.

At the committal proceedings were the usual figures, magistrate, police officers, lawyers, reporters and, of course, the accused prisoner. When Staff Sergeant Boshears appeared in court on Thursday, 5 January 1961, however, there was an extra character. This was Major Carl Prestin of the United States Judge Advocate's Department and he had a request to make which sounded to most of those in court like a piece of bare-faced effrontery. He suggested that under the Visiting Forces Act Boshears be remanded to an American detention facility and that they take over the case, removing it entirely from British jurisdiction!

The Chair of the magistrates, Lady Beatrice Plummer, was singularly unimpressed by the idea of the Americans taking over the prosecution, as were the police. The officer from the Judge Advocate's Department later tried going over their heads, but the Director of Public Prosecutions, Sir Theobald Matthew, also declined to consider the idea. Things could hardly have looked bleaker for Willie Boshears when he was tried for murder a few months later. But he had an ace up his sleeve. Despite the damning evidence against him, Boshears believed that he had a perfect defence to the charge of murder.

It should be mentioned that Willie Boshears was accused of a particularly unpleasant crime. Strangling the young woman was bad enough of course, but the courts, and indeed the general public, take a very dim view of killers who mutilate or otherwise interfere with the bodies of their victims. Hacking off and burning the hair, sticking the corpse in the bath to removed forensic evidence and then dumping it in a ditch like a bag of rubbish; all these things gave a very bad impression. It was hard to see how Boshears could hope to be acquitted when his trial began.

After he had pleaded 'not guilty' to the charge of murder, the prosecution presented their evidence, none of which was disputed by the defence. He had strangled the young woman and then, with shocking callousness, disposed of the corpse in a ditch. When the case for the defence opened, it was clear that they relied upon one simple, and exceedingly difficult to disprove, claim; Staff Sergeant Boshears had indeed choked Jean Constable to death, but he had done so in his sleep and had no recollection of the act. Once he woke up and found what had happened, he had panicked and so disposed of the body, fearing that nobody would ever believe his story. He was probably right about this, because the prosecution treated his account with incredulity. Nevertheless, he stuck to his version of events and it was left to the judge when summing up to express the view of most people on hearing this fantastic tale.

Mr Justice Glyn-Jones told the jury that they might assume that anybody putting his hands around somebody's throat and gripping with such force, for so long, must have intended either to inflict grievous bodily harm or cause death. He asked them, 'Have you ever heard of a man strangling a woman while he was sound asleep?' It was plain as a pikestaff what his own view on the subject was. The judge went on to say, 'We have no medical evidence that that there exists any record in all the records of the medical profession that such a thing has happened.' At this point, he paused and glared at the jury for a second or two, before continuing, 'You use your common sense and decide whether it happened.'

There can seldom have been a summing-up more hostile to a defendant and nobody in the court at Chelmsford that day seriously expected anything other than a swift verdict of 'guilty'. There were audible gasps of disbelief when, after less than two hours of deliberation, the jury returned to announce that they had acquitted Boshears of murder. He left the court a free man. The US Air Force though, had another view on the matter. That summer, he was discharged. In answer to queries about this move, the only reply was that his discharge had been, 'other than honourable'.

Actually, the judge had misdirected the jury, because there were a number of recognized cases of what is known as homicidal somnambulism. A famous incident in Glasgow in 1878 was that of Simon Fraser, a happily married man with an 18-month-old son. One night, Fraser got out of bed and, picking his son up, swung him round and dashed his brains out on the wall. Simon Fraser had a long history of carrying out bizarre acts while sleepwalking and as a consequence, he was acquitted of his son's murder. There have been a number of similar men who have been afflicted in the same way and in fairness, the judge at Boshears' trial should have pointed this out to the jury.

All of which brings us to the situation in the present day. What happens now if an American serviceman, or woman, commits a crime on British soil? Where does the jurisdiction now lie? The answer is complicated and the truth is that we simply do not know. The law itself is plain enough, but the governments of Britain and the United States have entered into a number of secret agreements which confer varying degrees of immunity on Americans working for their country in the United Kingdom.

After the death of Harry Dunn, the British Foreign Office advised the police that the driver of the car which killed him did not enjoy diplomatic immunity. By that time though, she had already been spirited out of the country. The fuss did not die down, as both the British and Americans hoped it would. Instead, more and more questions were asked, until a secret agreement came to light which shed light on the subject of American immunity from prosecution in Britain.

The RAF base in Northamptonshire is home to an American listening station. Twenty-five years ago, the Americans were very keen to expand this and bring in more staff. Most of these would be civilians and it was important to the United States that they should be protected from any inconvenience, such as being obliged to appear in British courts or anything of that sort. The letters between the Foreign Office and US Ambassador William J. Crowe, Jr cover the old idea that only staff actually on duty should be immune from the consequences of their actions and also explore the idea that immunity might be accorded to their families as well. The so-called 'Croughton Agreement', named after the RAF base, is open to various interpretations, especially as it has been amended since 1995. After the death of Harry Dunn, for instance, it was claimed that although immunity from prosecution had been withdrawn from staff working at RAF Croughton, it had, bizarrely, been retained for their families. At the time of writing, the summer of 2020, the Harry Dunn affair has not been resolved and there are doubtless new aspects of the case which will come to light in due course.

Endword

The situation relating to United States' forces in Britain between 1942 and 1945 is unique in British history. An army was garrisoned in the country which, legally, had licence to behave precisely as it wished with no possibility of any legal sanction being brought to bear for any reason whatsoever. Both Winston Churchill, the British Prime Minister, and President Roosevelt must have known that the only way that such a peculiar system would work was if the host country could be assured that any actions against the civilian population would be dealt with severely by the army itself. It was for this reason that the courts martial were held publicly and British civilians and newspaper reporters could attend and assure themselves that rapes, murders and other crimes were not being dealt with leniently. It was partly for that reason that the eighteen military executions at which we have looked were carried out. People in Britain knew that their own murderers were likely to be hanged and they needed to know that the same would apply to American soldiers. So much for the American occupation of the prison. What happened after they left?

Once the war in Europe ended in the early summer of 1945, there was little reason for the hundreds of thousands of American servicemen to remain in Britain. Some returned to the United States, while others were needed in the Far East, where the war with Japan was still being fought. There was certainly no longer any need for them to maintain a military prison in Britain and in September 1945 it was returned to the British Army, who, it will be recalled, had been using the place before the American arrived. For over 20 years Shepton Mallet functioned as a 'glasshouse', as British soldiers referred to their military prisons.

Perhaps the most famous prisoners at Shepton Mallet after the Americans left were the Kray Twins, notorious British gangsters. They were called up for military service in March 1952, but after reporting to their regiment at the Tower of London, they decided that army life was not for them and deserted. After being arrested by the Military Police, they were among the last people to be held prisoner in the Tower of London, which was the headquarters of the regiment to which they nominally belonged, the Royal Fusiliers. After more misbehaviour, they were remanded to Shepton Mallet to await their court martial, spending a month in the prison.

The army handed back the prison for civilian use in 1966 and it was used for both vulnerable prisoners, for example sex offenders who might be at risk in the general prison population, and first-time offenders. A year after it reopened as a civilian prison, the gallows were dismantled and the execution chamber turned into the prison library. Although the space where the trapdoor had been was boarded over, the hinges of the trapdoors were left *in situ* and they can be seen there today. Illustration 10 shows the remains of the trapdoors. For almost 50 years, Shepton Mallet went through various incarnations, being variously used as a training prison and to house those serving sentences of life imprisonment, before closing for good in 2013.

On 28 March 2013, a special closing ceremony was staged at Shepton Mallet Prison. The Bishop of Bath attended, as did members of the American armed forces. After it was closed, the prison became a museum, with guided tours available of the execution chamber and also the wall where two men were shot by firing squad. This is only a temporary arrangement though, for the building is due to be developed as, of all unlikely things, a block of luxury apartments. The centuries-old mellow stonework of the exterior walls might make such flats aesthetically appealing in appearance, once some of the more obvious features of its days as a prison, the barred windows and so on, have been removed. One suspects that the old and ugly execution chamber will be demolished when this redevelopment is undertaken. It is hard to imagine anybody wishing to use a room in which eighteen men were deliberately killed!

American Soldiers Executed in England between 1943 and 1945

Cobb, David; Private. Born 14/11/21
Hanged at Shepton Mallet Prison on 12/3/43, for the murder of Robert J. Cobner.

Smith, Harold A; Private. Born 4/1/23
Hanged at Shepton Mallet Prison on 26/6/43, for the murder of Harry M. Jenkins.

Davis, Lee A; Private. Born 8/1/23
Hanged at Shepton Mallet Prison on 14/12/43, for the murder of Cynthia June Lay and the rape of Muriel Fawden.

Waters, John H; Private. Born 1/10/05
Hanged at Shepton Mallet Prison on 10/2/44, for the murder of Doris May Staples.

Leatherberry, John C; Private. Born 19/1/22
Hanged at Shepton Mallet Prison on 16/5/44, for the murder of Harry Claude Hailstone.

Harris, Wiley Jnr; Private. Born 12/6/18
Hanged at Shepton Mallet Prison on 26/5/44, for the murder of Harry Coogan.

Miranda, Alex F; Private. Born 28/7/23
Shot by firing squad at Shepton Mallet Prison on 30/5/44, for the murder of Thomas Evison.

Brinson, Eliga; Private. Born 21/2/19
Hanged at Shepton Mallet Prison on 11/8/44, for the rape of Dorothy Holmes.

Smith, Willie; Private. Born 30/6/22
Hanged at Shepton Mallet Prison on 11/8/44, for the rape of Dorothy
  Holmes.

Thomas, Madison; Private. Born 3/3/21
Hanged at Shepton Mallet Prison on 12/10/44, for rape.

Pyegate, Benjamin; Private. Born 2/2/09
Shot by firing squad at Shepton Mallet Prison on 28/11/44, for the murder
  of James E. Alexander.

Clark, Ernest L; Corporal. Born 10/8/20
Hanged at Shepton Mallet Prison on 8/1/45, for the rape and murder of
  Betty Dorian Pearl Green.

Guerra, Augustine M; Private. Born 4/5/24
Hanged at Shepton Mallet Prison on 8/1/45, for the rape and murder of
  Betty Dorian Pearl Green.

Hulten, Karl; Private. Born 3/3/22
Hanged at Pentonville Prison on 8/3/45, for murder.

Jones, Cubia; Private. Born 12/5/19
Hanged at Shepton Mallet Prison on 17/3/45, for rape.

Pearson, Robert L; Corporal. Born 30/5/23
Hanged at Shepton Mallet Prison on 17/3/45, for rape.

Harrison, William Jr; Private. Born 27/7/22
Hanged at Shepton Mallet Prison on 7/4/45, or the rape and murder of
  Patricia Wylie.

Smith, George E. Jr: Private. Born 14/4/17
Hanged at Shepton Mallet Prison on 8/5/45, for the murder of Sir Eric
  Teichman.

Martinez, Aniceto; Private, First Class. Born 30/5/22
Hanged at Shepton Mallet Prison on 15/6/45, for rape.

Appendix 2

Where the Bodies are Buried

The disposal of the corpses of the eighteen men executed at Shepton Mallet Prison during the Second World War tells us a good deal about both the irrational regard in which the dead are held generally and the American attitude to their military dead in particular. The way in which the remains of people who have been executed are disposed of is an interesting study in its own right.

In Britain, during the years in which capital punishment was in use, the bodies of those hanged were buried in unmarked graves within the grounds of the prisons in which they died. They had no headstone to mark their final resting place and their relatives were not able to hold funerals to mark their death or visit the grave to lay flowers or anything of that kind. These men and women were, in effect, blotted out as though they had never lived. In a world which sets great store by the marking of births, marriages and deaths, this placed a heavy burden on the family of somebody who had been hanged. To use the modern expression, the lack of any funeral or other ceremony, such relatives were not able to effect 'closure'. This was a deliberate policy, a mark of society's disapprobation.

From time to time, corpses were retrieved from where they had been buried in prisons and given a proper and more reverent interment. This happened, for example, with Roger Casement, the Irishman who had been executed for treason in Pentonville Prison at the height of the First World War in 1916. In 1965, his corpse was exhumed from Pentonville Prison and returned to Ireland for an honourable burial. Rumours soon began to circulate though that the English had played a mean trick and that the corpse that they had sent to Ireland was not that of Roger Casement at all, but rather that of the murderer Dr Crippen! After these stories had gained strength for a few years, the British Home Secretary, James Callaghan, admitted in 1969 that Casement's body had been buried naked and quicklime poured into his grave. The hope had been that his remains would be utterly destroyed. As far as anybody could tell though, the body which had been sent back to Dublin had been the genuine article.

For the US Army in Britain, the question of where to place the bodies of those who had been hanged or shot after courts martial was complicated by the fact that they were resolutely determined that the United States alone should be responsible for its soldiers, whether living or dead. They thus hit upon a neat way both to ensure that the fact that these were Americans was acknowledged, while at the same time making perfectly sure that everybody would know that these men had died in disgrace, rather than on the battlefield.

There already existed an American military cemetery in England. This was situated in the Brookwood Cemetery, 30 miles from London. Sometimes known as the London Necropolis, Brookwood is the largest cemetery in Britain and one of the largest in the whole of Europe. After the end of the First World War, the United States established the Brookwood American Cemetery and Memorial here, where dead soldiers could be buried and those whose bodies could not be found had their names inscribed in a memorial chapel. When the Americans arrived in Britain in 1942, it seemed to them quite logical to carry on interring their war dead at Brookwood. The problem then arose about those who had been executed, rather than dying honourably in battle.

One point which had to be borne in mind was that before being executed, every one those men who had been hanged or shot at Shepton Mallet had first been dishonourably discharged from the US Army. In a sense, it would not be proper to bury them in an American military cemetery, because when they died they had not technically been serving members of the military. The alternative to letting them rest at Brookwood though would have been to allow then to be buried in a British civilian cemetery and we have seen how particular the Americans were about allowing their troops to be treated like anybody else in Britain. The solution was one of almost unbelievable pettiness and spite. The executed men would be buried in the American cemetery, but in ignominious circumstances.

Plot X was technically part of the American military cemetery, although at a little distance from the rest of the graves. It was a scrubby patch of land where the potting sheds and compost heap were to be found and it was there that the executed soldiers were laid, with no headstones, merely numbered markers. This was not consecrated ground, which added yet another touch to show the rejection of these men, and in a final show of contempt, they were buried not in coffins, but just shoved into old mattress covers. In effect, these men were segregated from their comrades for eternity. Except though, that they were not destined to spend eternity at Brookwood.

In addition to the American cemetery at Brookwood, there is another in France, dating from the First World War, called the Oise-Aisne American Cemetery and Memorial. Many of the American casualties of the Second World War were buried at a new site near Cambridge, on land donated by the university. At the end of the war the American Battle Monuments Commission decided that there should be a permanent cemetery at Cambridge for their soldiers who had died fighting in the war. This became the Cambridge American Cemetery and Memorial. Thomas B. Larkin, Quartermaster General of the US Army, directed that all those buried at Brookwood who had died fighting between 1942 and 1945 should be exhumed and then reburied at Cambridge. Those whose relatives wished, could have the bodies taken to the United States so that they might make other arrangements.

So it was that between January and May of 1948, a major operation took place, in the course of which all the American corpses from the Second World War at Brookwood were dug up and either taken to Cambridge or repatriated to the United States. This left the question of the disposal of the eighteen men who had been executed at Shepton Mallet. Nobody wanted them to buried with the real heroes at Cambridge, nor would they be left at Brookwood.

In the case of one of the eighteen men at Brookwood, the problem was solved by allowing the sister of David Cobb, the first man hanged at Shepton Mallet, to claim his body and have it returned to his home state of Alabama. For the remainder though, another solution would have to be found. It was a little troublesome and would entail transporting seventeen corpses across the English Channel. But on balance it appeared to the US Army to deal with the matter as neatly and expeditiously as could be.

At the Oise-Aisne American Cemetery and Memorial in France, a special plot, called Plot E, had been set aside for soldiers who had been executed. This area, where what are known officially as the 'dishonourable dead' are interred, is not mentioned on any material connected with the cemetery. The website says nothing of it, neither do any of the pamphlets available at the cemetery. It is clearly hoped that everybody will either forget about the men interred in Plot E or, failing that, will be tactful enough not to talk about it. Plot E may be seen in Illustration 20.

Plot E is outside the main part of the cemetery and is surrounded by privet hedges. Bizarrely, there is no entrance to it. One has to enquire at the cemetery superintendent's office and a rear door from the office provides the only access. There are no gravestones in Plot E, just tiny little plaques, bearing not names, but numbers. If you want to find a specific grave, you have to consult the superintendent. In this space are all the men who were executed in Europe following courts martial. Eddie Slovik, the only American soldier executed for desertion since the American Civil War, was buried here. Permission was gained from his family in 1988 to have his body taken back to the United States and given a proper burial. It was here that the seventeen bodies dug up from Brookwood were brought in 1948 and buried alongside the other 'dishonourable dead'. Only sixteen of the men executed at Shepton Mallet now remain here, because as we saw in the chapter on Alex Miranda, his remains were repatriated to the United States in 1990.

Appendix 3

The Executioners at Shepton Mallet, 1943–1945

Thomas William Pierrepoint 1870–1954

Thomas Pierrepoint was born to a working-class family in the English county of Nottinghamshire. He had a number of brothers and sisters, including Henry, who was born eight years later. Henry Pierrepoint had a childhood ambition to be a hangman and when he was 24, he wrote to the Home Secretary asking if he could be considered for the post. After training at Strangeways Prison in Manchester, Henry, who was generally known as 'Harry', was accepted as an assistant executioner. Although the fees which he was paid were not vast, they provided a reasonable supplementary income and also gave the young man the opportunity to travel around the country at the government's expense.

Within only a few short years, Harry Pierrepoint had been promoted to the position of 'Number One', that is to say as having responsibility for carrying out executions himself, with the aid of an assistant. It struck him that he could not hope for a better assistant than his older brother Thomas and so he undertook to train him himself in the art of hanging. Thomas Pierrepoint had had up to that time various careers, including farmer, haulier and bookmaker. In 1905, he was working in a quarry, while his wife ran a shop. Harry Pierrepoint trained his brother in how to hang a man by means of a rope rigged up in a barn at the back of his sister-in-law's shop! He underwent a mandatory course arranged at London's Pentonville Prison afterwards, but it was clear to the staff there that he already knew as much as they did about hanging. On 9 April 1906, Tom Pierrepoint travelled with his brother to the Yorkshire town of Wakefield to execute a man called James McConnell, who had been convicted of murdering his wife in circumstances of the utmost brutality. Harry and Tom Pierrepoint worked well together as a team and over the course of the next four years hanged a total of twenty-five men, always with the older brother assisting the younger.

Harry Pierrepoint's career as a hangman came to an abrupt end in July 1910, which had the effect of boosting his brother's prospects in that field enormously. On 13 July that year, Harry Pierrepoint travelled to Chelmsford Prison in Essex to hang a man called Frederick Foreman, who had beaten his girlfriend to death. Instead of having his brother to assist him, Pierrepoint had been assigned a man called John Ellis, whom he detested. Arriving at the prison smelling of drink, Harry Pierrepoint proceeded to pick a fight with Ellis and a warder was compelled to step in and separate the two men. Although the hanging, carried out the following morning at eight, went off smoothly, John Ellis lodged a complaint with the Home Office about Pierrepoint's conduct. Since the warders at Chelmsford Prison backed up Ellis's account and agreed that Harry Pierrepoint had been drunk when he got to the prison, the Home Office decided not to use his services again.

The sudden loss of such a capable and experienced executioner meant that there was now a shortage of men who could officiate as 'chief', that is to say, actually undertake the business of calculating the drop, rigging up the rope and so on. For this reason, although he had only four years' record as an assistant, Tom Pierrepoint was asked to carry out a hanging in Yorkshire just four weeks after his brother had effectively been sacked. On that date, he hanged a man at Leeds Prison who had been convicted of murdering his wife.

For the next 35 years, Tom Pierrepoint was to be the undisputed chief executioner in Britain. In total, he took part in one capacity or another in an astonishing 294 hangings. It was a record only to be surpassed by his nephew Albert, Harry Pierrepoint's son. It was Albert Pierrepoint who assisted his uncle with almost all the executions at Shepton Mallet.

By the time that he began hanging American soldiers at Shepton Mallet, Tom Pierrepoint was in his seventies and a number of those who saw him in action during the Second World War thought that he was getting too old for the job. He may be seen in Illustration 11. He had always been of the opinion that the sooner the condemned man was out of his cell and standing on the scaffold, the better for all concerned. It was better for the victim, because the whole thing was over and done with swiftly, often in a matter of seconds. It was better too for those taking part, because it lessened the chance of the condemned prisoner fainting or starting a fight. As soon as he entered the cell, Pierrepoint would strap the man or woman's wrists behind their back and then march the individual briskly to the scaffold. Several people though complained that as the executioner grew older, he became even more brusque and even little callous. Had it not been wartime, which made it tricky to find a replacement for him, it seems likely that Tom Pierrepoint's retirement would have been engineered and his nephew allowed to take over as the chief executioner in Britain.

By the time that the war ended, Tom Pierrepoint was almost crippled with arthritis and needed a stick to get about. He turned 75 in October 1945 and yet, almost unbelievably, he was still being called upon to hang people. Letters were by now being exchanged on a regular basis between concerned prison governors and the Home Office, enquiring for how much longer this old man was to be allowed to continue his duties. On 28 May 1946 Pierrepoint hanged a man at Lincoln and this was to be the last execution which he was to undertake in England. On 10 August 1946, just two months before his 76th birthday, Tom Pierrepoint was asked to hang a man at Glasgow's Barlinnie Prison. Although he did not know it, this was to be the last execution in which he was to be involved. Forty years after he had first assisted his brother in hanging a man, the Home Office finally decided that it was time to let the old man go. He lived for another eight years, dying at his daughter's home in 1954.

Albert Pierrepoint 1905–1992
When Albert Pierrepoint was 11 years old, he and the other children in his class at school were set a composition to write, on the subject of

what they wanted to be when they grew up. All the other little boys wished to be train drivers or explorers. Albert's ambition was to be a hangman. Perhaps this was not all that surprising, when you consider that both his father and uncle were hangmen.

As we saw above, Albert Pierrepoint's father lost his position as executioner when his son was just five, but his Uncle Tom was to continue in the trade for another 36 years. The youngster was perfectly aware of what his uncle did regularly and there was nothing that young Albert wanted more than to follow in his uncle's footsteps.

When he left school, Albert Pierrepoint worked at several different jobs before settling down to work for a wholesale grocer. In April 1931, without telling his uncle what he was doing, Albert wrote the following letter;

The Prison Commissioners
Home Office
London

19/4/31

Dear Sir,
I beg to offer you my services as an Assistant executioner to my uncle T.W. Pierrepoint at any time he or any other retire from their position. My age is 26 and I am strong in health and build. During the last few years I have thoroughly studied the carrying out of an execution and the calculating of drops etc. learned from the diary of my late father Mr H.A. Pierrepoint. Hoping this letter will meet your kind approval.

I am dear Sir,
Your obedient servant
Albert Pierrepoint.

Although there was no current vacancy, Pierrepoint's name was put on a waiting list. The fact that he was the nephew of the country's foremost hangman must surely have been borne in mind, because six months later he was invited to an interview at Manchester's Strangeways Prison. That spring he was then offered the opportunity to attend a training course in Pentonville Prison in London.

Harry Pierrepoint had, on his death, left a large collection of papers relating to the period when he was a hangman. In addition to this, he had kept a meticulous professional diary of all his engagements. Albert Pierrepoint had studied these carefully over the years, as well as talking a great deal to his uncle about the subject of hanging. By the time that he arrived at Pentonville in April 1932, he already knew more than most people about the technique of hanging as it was practised in Britain.

Following his successful completion of the course on judicial hanging, it was to be another three months before Albert Pierrepoint had the opportunity to take part in an execution. His uncle invited him to travel to Dublin to assist him in an execution there. Although Ireland was now an independent country, they still preferred to use British executioners rather than training their own. On Tuesday, 27 December 1932, uncle and nephew travelled to Ireland by boat to execute a man called Patrick McDermott, who had murdered his own brother.

The execution, on 29 December, went very smoothly, with Albert Pierrepoint's contribution being limited to buckling a strap around the condemned man's ankles once he was standing on the drop. After the hanging was over, somebody produced a bottle of whiskey and offered a glass to all those present. Tom Pierrepoint declined firmly and indicated to his nephew by a look that he too should refuse. On the ferry back to England, his uncle told Albert that if one couldn't do the job without whiskey, then one should not do it at all. He was presumably thinking of his brother's ignominious fall from the position of chief.

Over the next 10 years Albert Pierrepoint assisted his uncle at dozens of executions. It was to be nine years after that first execution before he was given the opportunity to carry out a hanging as 'Number One', rather than merely assisting. This was at the execution of a gangster called Antonio Mancini, known to his associates as 'Babe'. He stabbed another criminal who was trying to operate a protection racket on the club which Mancini ran. He met his death bravely, for as he was standing on the gallows and the noose was being placed about his neck, he smiled and said, 'Cheerio!' casually.

It was perhaps inevitable that Albert Pierrepoint should assist his uncle at eleven of the sixteen executions which took place at Shepton Mallet Prison during the Second World War. That he was not present at every one of the hangings was due to the fact that he was now in demand in his own right as an executioner not only in Britain, but also in Germany. Albert Pierrepoint hanged many of the war criminals who had been convicted of atrocities in concentration camps, such as the staff from Belsen. With Tom Pierrepoint's enforced retirement in 1946, his nephew became the most prominent hangman in the country, participating in a total of 435 executions. He gave up the position in 1956, following a dispute about the fee owing to him after he travelled to a prison, only to find that the man had been reprieved. Albert Pierrepoint may be seen in Illustration 12.

Bibliography

Abbot, Geoffrey (1995), *Book of Execution: An Encyclopedia of Methods of Judicial Execution*, London, Headline Publishing.

Allen, Howard W. (2009), *Race, Class, and the Death Penalty: Capital Punishment in American History*, New York, State University of New York Press.

Bakken, Gordon Morris (2010), *Invitation to an Execution: A History of the Death Penalty in the United States*, Albuquerque, University of New Mexico Press.

Clarke, John M. (2018), *London's Necropolis: A Guide to Brookwood Cemetery*, Catrine, Stenlake Publishing.

Disney, Francis (1992), *Shepton Mallet Prison*, New York, Hyperion Books.

Drimmer, Frederick (2014), *Executions in America: Over Three Hundred Years of Crime and Capital Punishment in America*, New York, Skyhorse Publishing.

Duff, Charles (1928), *A Handbook on Hanging*, London, Cayme Press.

Eddleston, John J. (2004), *The Encyclopaedia of Executions*, London, John Blake Publishing.

Fielding, Steve (2006), *Pierrepoint: A Family of Executioners*, London, John Blake Publishing.

Fielding, Steve (2008), *The Executioner's Bible*, London, John Blake Publishing.

Gunnarsson, Robert L. (2011), *American Military Police in Europe, 1945–1991: Unit Histories*, Jefferson, McFarland Books.

Holt, Dean W. (1992), *American Military Cemeteries: A Comprehensive Illustrated Guide to the Hallowed Grounds of the United States, Including Cemeteries Overseas*, Jefferson, McFarland.

Jay, Antony (ed.) (1996), *The Oxford Dictionary of Political Quotations*, Oxford, Oxford University Press.

Klein, Leonora (2006), *A Very English Hangman: The Life and Times of Albert Pierrepoint*, London, Corvo Books.

Moore, William (1974), *The Thin Yellow Line*, London, Leo Cooper.

O'Brien, John Paul Jones (2019), *A Treatise on American Military Laws, and the Practice of Courts Martial: With Suggestions for Their Improvement*, Stockbridge MA, Hardpress Publishing.

Opinions (1945), *European Theater of Operations, Board of Review*, Washington, Office of the Judge Advocate General.

Orwell, George (1965), *Decline of the English Murder and Other Essays*, London, Penguin Books.

Pierrepoint, Albert (1974), *Executioner: Pierrepoint*, London, Harrap.

Reynolds, David (2000), *Rich Relations: The American Occupation of Britain, 1942-1945*, London, Phoenix Press.

Reynolds, David (2009), *America, Empire of Liberty*, London, Allen Lane.

Roland, Paul (2012), *The Nuremberg Trials*, London, Arcturus Publishing.

Smith, Graham (1987), *When Jim Crow Met John Bull: Black American Soldiers in World War II Britain*, London, Taurus.

Stone, Allen (2005), *Shepton Mallet: A Visible History*, Shepton Mallet, Shepton Mallet Local History Society.

Taylor, A.J.P (1963), *The First World War*, London, Hamish Hamilton.

Webb, Simon (2016), *British Concentration Camps*, Barnsley, Pen and Sword History.

Webb, Simon (2012), *Execution: A History of Capital Punishment in Britain*, Stroud, The History Press.

Index